ALL-AMERICAN BLUES - COMPLETE 144 Songs

Catalog #07-1096

ISBN# 1-56922-036-0

Printed in the United States of America

Produced by John L. Haag

Exclusive Selling Agent:
CREATIVE CONCEPTS PUBLISHING CORP.
410 Bryant Circle, Box 848, Ojai, California 93024

CONTENTS

CONTENTS

BIG BILL BROONZY

SLIM HARPO

ELMORE JAMES

PAUL BUTTERFIELD

MUDDY WATERS

SONNY TERRY

BROWNIE MC GHEE

MEMPHIS SLIM

JOHNNY SHINES

JIMMY REED

CLIFTON CHENIER

HOWLIN' WOLF

SMILEY LEWIS

LILLIAN "LIL" GREEN

OTIS SPANN

JIMMY MC CRACKLIN

MANCE LIPSCOMB

JOHN MAYALL

CHARLES BROWN

"BLIND" LEMON JEFFERSON

GUITAR SLIM

JOHN LEE HOOKER

RICHIE HAVENS

BUDDY GUY

LIGHTNIN' SLIM

LIGHTNIN' HOPKINS

JIMMY COTTON

HUDDIE LEDBETTER (LEADBELLY)

ALBERT COLLINS

LOWELL FULSON

"MISSISSIPPI" JOHN HURT

SUNNYLAND SLIM

MISSISSIPPI FRED MC DOWELL

CHAMPION JACK DUPREE

LOUIS JORDAN

MA RAINEY

LITTLE MILTON

AARON "T-BONE" WALKER

BO DIDDLEY

SONNY BOY WILLIAMSON II

BOBBY "BLUE" BLAND

EDDIE "SON" HOUSE

REV. "BLIND" GARY DAVIS

HOWLIN' WOLF

BESSIE SMITH

LUTHER ALLISON

SKIPPY JAMES

B.B. KING

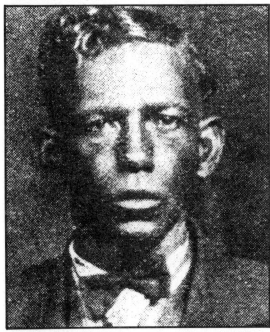

CHARLEY PATTON

ALBERT KING

ARTHUR "BIG BOY" CRUDUP

PERCY MAYFIELD

JIMMY REED

BIG BILL BROONZY

JIMMY YANCEY

BUDDY GUY

WILLIE DIXON

JIMMY WITHERSPOON

JOHN LEE HOOKER

CHAMPION JACK DUPREE

MUDDY WATERS

KOKOMO ARNOLD

AMOS MILBURN

JAMES ODEN (ST. LOUIS JIMMY)

BUDDY GUY

MEMPHIS MINNIE

BIG JOE WILLIAMS

LIGHTNING HOPKINS

B.B. KING

SONNY BOY WILLIAMSON II

ANDREW "SMOKEY" HOGG

LITTLE WALTER

EDDIE "CLEANHEAD" VINSON

FREDDIE KING

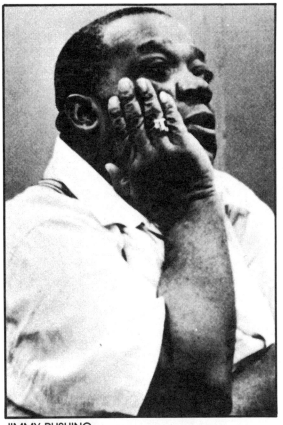

JIMMY RUSHING

MANCE LIPSCOMB with SON HOUSE

SONNY TERRY

JUNIOR WELLS

T-BONE WALKER

JOSH WHITE

ARTHUR "BIG BOY" CRUDUP

ROOSEVELT SYKES

GEORGIA TOM

BROWNIE McGHEE

22

After Hours

I WAS SIT·TIN' DOWN HERE THINK·IN'— ALL IN MY LONE·SOME CELL,—

I WAS JUST THINK·IN' AND WON·D'RIN'— THINK·IN' AND WON·D'RIN— ALL TO MY·

SELF.———— IT WAS AFTER HOURS———— IT WAS

AF·TER EV·'RY·THING WAS CLOSED, I BE·GAN LOOK·IN' A·ROUND,

WON·D'RIN' WHERE COULD—— MY BA·BY GO.

I'M GOIN' TO TELL YOU, BABY, SOMETHIN' I DON'T LIKE,
THE WAY YOU TREAT ME HERE YOU HAVE TO CUT IT OUT.
SOME OLD DAY IT'LL BE AFTER HOURS, I'LL COME WALKING IN,
AND I'LL KNOW, BABY, IF THINGS AIN'T RIGHT LIKE THEY SHOULD HAVE
BEEN.

I'M GONNA TELL YOU SOMETHIN', BABY, THAT YOU AIN'T GONNA LIKE,
IF I QUIT YOU THIS TIME, AIN'T GONNA TAKE YOU BACK.
I'M GONNA LEAVE YOU HERE AND ALL ALONE,
I'M COMIN' BACK TO SEE MY HAPPY HOME.

© 1978 ROAD ISLAND CO.— ALL RIGHTS RESERVED.

Ain't Gonna Let Nobody Turn Me Around

Appetite Blues

BY LIGHTNIN' SAM HOPKINS

THE WO·MAN THAT I LOVE   YOU KNOW SHE TAKES MY AP·PE·TITE____

THE WO·MAN THAT I AM LOV·ING____

YOU KNOW SHE TAKES MY AP·PE·TITE____   YOU KNOW THAT IS THE

CUTEST LIT·TLE WO·MAN____   I MOST EV·ER SEEN IN MY

LIFE____

BABY, PLEASE COME HOME

By James Moore

Baby, Please Don't Go

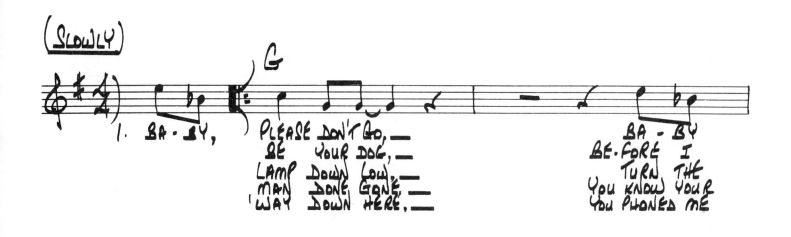

BABY, SCRATCH MY BACK

By James Moore

BLUES (SPOKEN:)

F

"AW, I'M ITCHIN' AND I DON'T KNOW WHERE TO SCRATCH.

Bb9 · F

COME HERE, BABY SCRATCH MY BACK. I KNOW YOU CAN

C7 · Bb9 · F · (GUITAR TACET)

DO IT, SO, BABY, GET TO IT. AW. YOU'RE WORKING WITH IT NOW.

F9

YOU GOT ME FEELIN' SO GOOD. LOOK HOW IT'S DONE

Bb7 · Ab/Bb · F7

C7 · Bb9 · F · Eb · Db · Gb7 · F

NOW YOU'RE DOIN' THE CHICKEN SCRATCH BABY, SCRATCH MY BACK."

Back Door Friend

By Stan Lewis & Lightnin' Sam Hopkins

1) What are you gon-na do with a wo-man _____
2)   It's hard to love a wo-man _____

When she's got a back-door friend _____
When she's got a back-door friend _____

What are you gon-na do with a wo-man _____
It's hard to love a wo-man _____

When she's got a back-door friend _____
When she's got a back-door friend _____

She's just pray-in' for you to move out _____
When she's pray-in' for you to move out _____

So her back-door friend can move in _____
So her back-door friend can move in _____

Back Water Blues

1. WELL IT RAINED FIVE DAYS AND THE SKY WAS DARK AS NIGHT,_____
_____ YES, IT RAINED FIVE DAYS AND THE SKY WAS DARK AS NIGHT,_____ THERE'S
TROU·BLE IN____ THE LOW____ LANDS TO·NIGHT._____

2. I GOT UP ONE MORNIN', I COULDN'T EVEN GET OUT OF MY DOOR,
   I GOT UP EARLY ONE MORNIN', I COULDN'T EVEN GET OUT OF MY DOOR,
   THAT WAS ENOUGH TROUBLE TO MAKE A POOR BOY WONDER WHERE TO GO
   (CHORUS:)

3. I WENT AND I STOOD UP ON A HIGH OLD LONESOME HILL,
   YOU KNOW I WENT AND I STOOD UP ON A HIGH OLD LONESOME HILL,
   I DID ALL I COULD DO TO LOOK DOWN ON THE HOUSE WHERE I USED TO
                                                              LIVE.
   (CHORUS:)

4. IT THUNDERED AND LIGHTNIN'ED, AND THE WIND BEGAN TO BLOW,
   "   "   "   "   "   "   "   "   "   "
   THERE WERE THOUSANDS OF POOR PEOPLE DIDN'T HAVE NO PLACE TO GO

Bad Breaks

By: B. B. King, J. Josea
and S. Ling

(Moderately, with Soul)

OH! I WISH I WAS SIN-GLE, 'CAUSE MY WO-MAN, SHE DRIVES ME MAD ____ I WISH I WAS SIN-GLE, 'CAUSE MY WO-MAN, SHE DRIVES ME MAD ____ YES, SHE'S AL-WAYS AC-CUS-ING ME OF SOME-ONE SOME-ONE I AIN'T NEV-ER HAD ____

LAST NIGHT I FELT LUCKY BUT MY LUCK WAS RUNNING SLOW
THE LAST HAND I CAUGHT FOUR ACES AND THE POLICE BROKE DOWN THE DOOR
I SAID, "LORD, LORD, WHAT CAN A POOR BOY DO"?
IT'S TOUGH WHEN YOU CAN'T MAKE NO MONEY
SEEMS LIKE ALL THE BAD BREAKS COME TO YOU.

3. GOT HOME THIS MORNING
SHE WAS LOOKING KINDA FUNNY
SHE SAID "DON'T COME IN HERE, DADDY,
UNLESS YOU GOT SOME MONEY"
I SAID LORD . . . etc.

4. I ASKED MY WOMAN FOR SOME DINNER
SHE LOOKED AT ME LIKE A FOOL
SHE SAID "I'M PLAYING CHECKERS, DADDY,
AND I THINK IT'S YOUR TIME TO MOVE
I SAID LORD . . . etc.

BAD LUCK BLUES

I WAN·NA GO HOME AND I AIN'T GOT___ SUF·FI·CIENT

CLOTHES (DOG·GONE MY BAD·LUCK SOUL) WAN·NA GO HOME AND___ I AIN'T GOT SUF·

FI·CIENT CLOTHES,___ I MEAN SUF·FI·CIENT COLD WEATH·ER CLOTHES, WELL, I

WAN·NA GO HOME AND I AIN'T GOT SUF·FI·CIENT CLOTHES. (I BET MY)

I BET MY MONEY AND I LOST IT, LORD, IT'S GONE (DOGGONE MY BAD·LUCK SOUL);
MMM___ LOST IT, LORD, IT'S GONE,
I MEAN, LOST IT___ YEARS AGO,
I'LL NEVER BET ON THE QUEEN OF SPADES NO MORE.

WELL, MY GOOD GAL LEFT TOWN___ WHY·DON'T YOU QUIT CRYIN'? (DOGGON MY BAD·LUCK SOUL);
MMM___ WHY DON'T YOU QUIT CRYIN'?
WHY DON'T YOU QUIT___ I MEAN___ CRYIN'?
THAT JOKER STOLE OFF WITH THAT LONG·HAIRED GAL OF MINE.

SUGAR, YOU CATCH THE KATY AND I'LL CATCH THAT SANTY FE (E) (DOGGONE MY BAD·LUCK SOUL);
SUGAR, YOU CATCH THE KATY, I'LL CATCH THE SANTY FE (E),
I MEAN, SANTY___ SING ABOUT FE (E);
WHEN YOU GET TO DENVER, PRETTY MAMA, LOOK AROUND FOR ME.

THE WOMAN I LOVE IS FIVE FEET FROM THE GROUND (DOGGONE MY BAD·LUCK SOUL);
HEY, FIVE FEET FROM THE GROUND,
HEY___ FIVE FEET FROM THE___ I MEAN GROUND,
SHE'S A TAILOR·MADE WOMAN, SHE AIN'T NO HAND·ME·DOWN.

BAD LUCK AND TROUBLE

BY LIGHTNIN SAM HOPKINS
& JULES TAUB

TICKET AGENT

BY LIGHTNIN' SAM HOPKINS

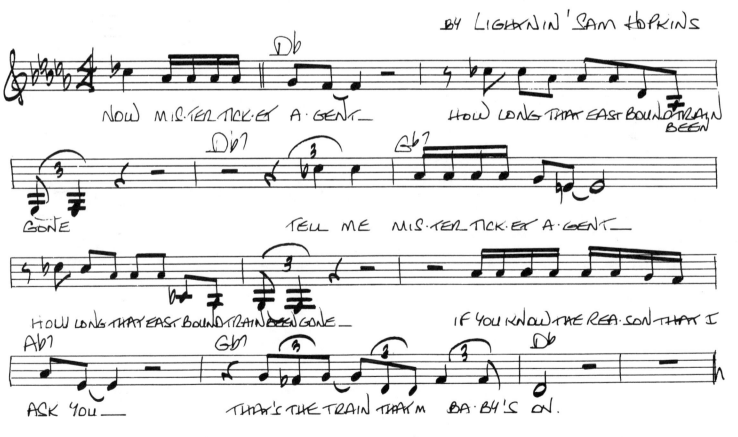

Black Cat

By Lightnin' Sam Hopkins

Well you're one black cat some-day you'll find your tree _____

_____ Well you're one black cat some-day you'll find your

tree _____ Then I'll hide my shoe

Some-where near your cher-ry tree _____
Well I
Well I
Well I

Take you down in town   I paid your doc-tor bill   when
Took you in my home   you ate up all my bread   I
Woke up this mor-nin'   the same thing on my mind   I was

I'm in some trou-ble, _____ you're try-in' to get me killed
Left there this mor-nin' _____ you tried to mess up in my bed   {Well you're
Thinkin' 'bout you ba-by _____ you were walkin' down the line}

One black cat some-day you'll find your tree _____ Then I'll

Hide my shoe some-where near your cher-ry tree. _____

The Blues Ain't Nothin'

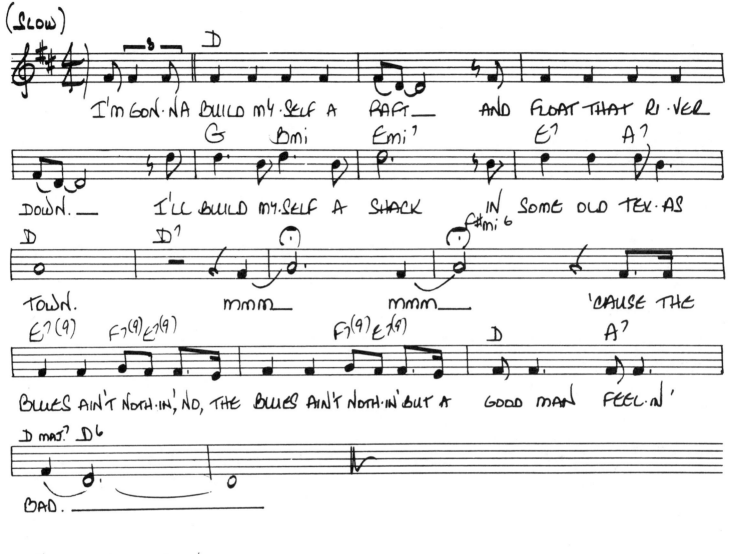

(Slow)

I'm gon-na build my-self a raft___ and float that ri-ver
down.___ I'll build my-self a shack in some old Tex-as
town. mmm___ mmm___ 'cause the
blues ain't noth-in', no, the blues ain't noth-in' but a good man feel-in'
bad.___

I'm goin' down on the levee,
goin' down to take myself a rockin' chair.
If my lovin' gal don't come,
I rock away from there.
mmm _ mmm . . .
'cause the blues ain't nothin', but a good man feelin' bad.

Why did you leave me blue?
Why did you leave me blue?
All I can do is sit
and cry and cry for you.
mmm _ mmm . . . 'cause the blues ain't nothin',
no, the blues ain't nothin',
but a good man feelin' bad.

Blues For My Man

2. OH, WHEN A WOMAN GET BLUE, HANG HER HEAD AND SHE CRY,
   " " " " " " " " " " " " " " "
   BUT WHEN A MAN GET BLUE, HE GRAB A TRAIN AND RIDE.

3. I WISH MY MAN WOULD COME BACK 'CAUSE I LOVE HIM SO BAD,
   I WISH MY MAN WOULD COME BACK 'CAUSE I LOVE HIM SO BAD,
   AND IF HE DON'T COME BACK, I'LL KEEP A-FEELIN' SAD.

4. I THINK I'LL TAKE ME A WALK BY THE RIVER SO DEEP,
   " " " " " " " " " " " " " " "
   I'M GONNA GO ON IN, I'M GONNA STAY FOR KEEPS.

Blues Hang-Over

By James Moore
and Jerry West

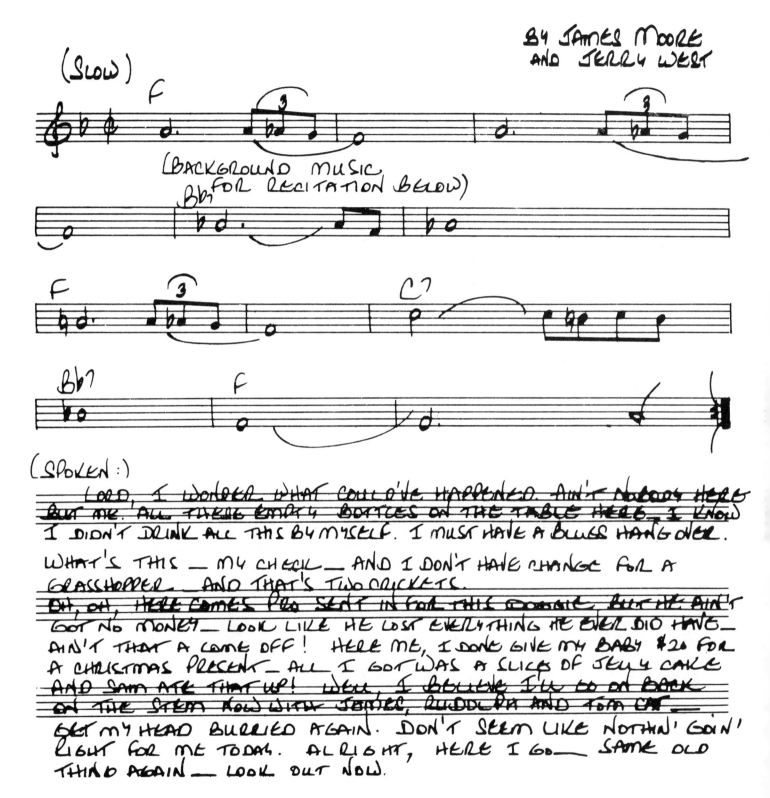

(Spoken:)

Lord, I wonder what could've happened. Ain't nobody here but me. All these empty bottles on the table here. I know I didn't drink all this by myself. I must have a blues hang over. What's this — my check — and I don't have change for a grasshopper. And that's two crickets. Oh, oh, here comes Leo sent in for this domain but he ain't got no money. Look like he lost everything he ever did have. Ain't that a come off! Hear me, I done give my baby $20 for a Christmas present. All I got was a slice of jelly cake and Sam ate that up! Well, I believe I'll go on back on the stem now with Janice, Rudolph and Tom Cat. Get my head burried again. Don't seem like nothin' goin' right for me today. Alright, here I go — same old thing again — look out now.

BREAKFAST TIME

BY LIGHTNIN' SAM HOPKINS

COOK MY BREAK·FAST   BRING IT TO___ MY   BED___

COOK MY BREAK·FAST   BRING IT TO___ MY

BED   WHEN I   EAT   THIS

MORN·ING   MY   WHOLE FAM'LY BEEN   FED.   (SPOKEN)

2) COOK MY BISCUITS — COOK 'EM GOOD AND BROWN
   COOK MY BISCUITS — COOK 'EM GOOD AND BROWN
   IF YOU SEE MY BREAD BURNING
   TURN YOUR PAN AROUND.

3) I WANT MY COFFEE — I WANT IT HOT, HOT
   I WANT MY COFFEE — I WANT IT HOT, I WANT IT HOT
   I WANT YOU TO TURN UP YOUR STOVE
   SO IT WILL BURN MY COFFEE HOT.

BROKE AND HUNGRY

I ___ AM BROKE AND HUNGRY, RAGG'D AND DIR·TY TOO. ___ I SAY I'M BROKE AND HUN·GRY, ___ RAG·G'D AND DIR·TY TOO. ___ IF I CLEAN UP ___ CAN I GO HOME WITH YOU? ___ I ___

2. I AM MOTHERLESS, FATHERLESS, SISTER AND BROTHERLESS TOO.
I SAY I'M " " " " " " " " " "
REASON I TRIED SO HARD TO MAKE THIS TRIP WITH YOU.

3. YOU MISS ME, WOMAN, COUNT THE DAYS I'M GONE.
" " " " " " " " " " "
I'M GOIN' AWAY TO BUILD ME A RAILROAD OF MY OWN.

4. I FEEL LIKE JUMPIN' THROUGH THE KEYHOLE IN YOUR DOOR.
" " " " " " " "
IF YOU JUMP THIS TIME, BABY, YOU WON'T JUMP NO MORE.

5. I BELIEVE MY GOOD GAL HAS FOUND MY BLACK CAT BONE.
I SAY I B'LIEVE " " " " " " " " "
I CAN LEAVE SUNDAY MORNING; MONDAY MORNING I'M STICKIN' 'ROUND

6. I WANT TO SHOW YOU WOMEN WHAT CARELESS LOVE HAS DONE. | Home.
" " " " " " " " "
CAUSE A MAN LIKE ME TO BE 'WAY, 'WAY FROM HOME.

Brown's Ferry Blues

OPEN A TUNING

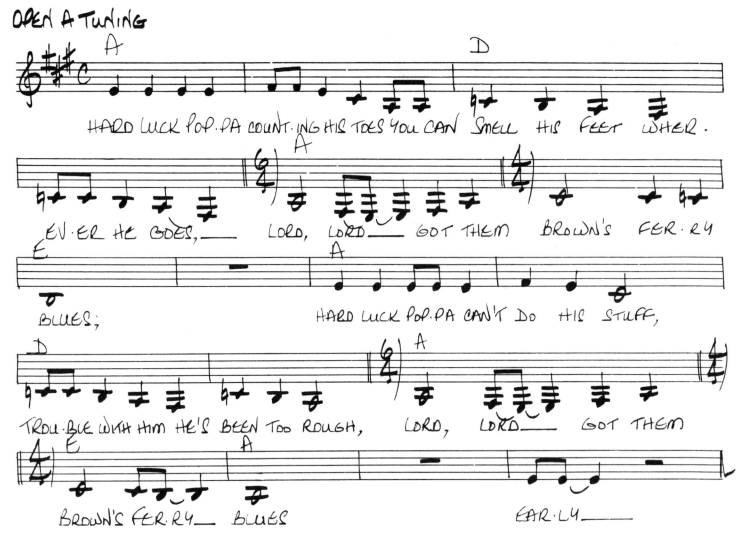

HARD LUCK POP-PA COUNT-ING HIS TOES YOU CAN SMELL HIS FEET WHER-

EV-ER HE GOES,___ LORD, LORD___ GOT THEM BROWN'S FER-RY

BLUES; HARD LUCK POP-PA CAN'T DO HIS STUFF,

TROU-BLE WITH HIM HE'S BEEN TOO ROUGH, LORD, LORD___ GOT THEM

BROWN'S FER-RY___ BLUES EAR-LY___

2. EARLY TO BED AND EARLY TO RISE
AND YOUR GIRL GOES OUT WITH OTHER GUYS,
LORD, LORD GOT THEM BROWN'S FERRY BLUES.

3. IF YOU DON'T BELIEVE ME TRY IT YOURSELF
WELL I TRIED, AND I GOT LEFT,
LORD, LORD GOT THEM BROWN'S FERRY BLUES.

4. HARD LUCK POPPA STANDING IN THE RAIN
IF THE WORLD WAS CORN, HE COULDN'T BUY GRAIN,
LORD, LORD GOT THEM BROWN'S FERRY BLUES.

Buzz Me Babe

By James Moore
and Jerry West

(1.) You buzz me, babe, on your tel-e-phone,

You buzz me, babe, on your tel-e-phone,

Want to know from you, ba-by, that stay-in' still goin' on.

(2.) While I'm young, babe, and I'm feel-in' fine,
(3.) When I'm old, babe, and can't stand no more,

While I'm young, babe, and I'm feel-in' fine,
When I'm old, babe, and can't stand no more,

Wan-na love you, ba-by, while I've still got time. _____
Wan-na love you, ba-by, then I'll let you go. _____

BUDDY WON'T YOU ROLL DOWN THE LINE

WAY BACK YON·DER IN TEN·NES·SEE, THEY LEASED THE CON·VICTS OUT, THEY

WORKED THEM IN THE COAL MINES A·GAINST FREE LA·BOR STOUT, FREE

LA·BOR RE·BELLED A·GAINST IT, TO WIN IT TOOK SOME TIME, BUT

WHILE THE LEASE WAS IN EF·FECT THEY MADE 'EM RISE AND SHINE. OH, BUD·DY WON'T YOU

ROLL DOWN THE LINE, BUD·DY WON'T YOU ROLL DOWN THE LINE,

YON·DER COMES MY DAR·LIN' COM· IN' DOWN THE LINE, BUD·DY WON'T YOU

ROLL DOWN THE LINE, BUD·DY WON'T YOU ROLL DOWN THE LINE,

YON·DER COMES MY DAR·LIN' COM·IN' DOWN THE LINE.

(SPOKEN :)

2. A·OH, COMIN' UP HARD
   WAY BACK YONDER IN TENNESSEE,
   THEY LEASED THE CONVICTS OUT,
   THEY WORKED THEM IN THE COAL MINES
   AGAINST FREE LABOR STOUT.
   FREE LABOR REBELLED AGAINST IT,
   TO WIN IT TOOK SOME TIME,
   BUT WHILE THE LEASE WAS IN EFFECT,
   THEY MADE 'EM RISE AND SHINE.

        · CHORUS ·

3. EARLY MONDAY MORNING,
   GOT 'EM OUT ON TIME,
   MARCH YOU DOWN TO LONE ROCK,
   JUST TO LOOK INTO THAT MINE.
   MARCH YOU DOWN TO LONE ROCK,
   JUST TO LOOK INTO THAT HOLE,
   VERY LAST WORD THE CAPTAIN SAY:
   "YOU'D BETTER GET YOUR POLE."

        · CHORUS ·

4. THE BEANS THEY ARE HALF·DONE,
   THE BREAD IS NOT SO WELL,
   THE MEAT IT IS BURNT UP,
   AND THE COFFEE'S BLACK AS HECK.
   BUT WHEN YOU GET YOUR TASKS DONE,
   YOU'RE GLAD TO COME TO CALL,
   FOR ANYTHING YOU GET TO EAT,
   IT TASTES GOOD DONE OR RAW.

        · CHORUS ·

5. THE BANK BOSS IS A HARD MAN,
   A MAN YOU ALL KNOW WELL,
   AND IF YOU DON'T GET YOUR TASK DONE,
   HE'S GONNA GIVE YOU HALLELUJAH.
   CARRY YOU TO THE STOCKADE,
   AND ON THE FLOOR YOU'LL FALL,
   VERY NEXT TIME THEY CALL ON YOU,
   YOU'D BETTER HAVE YOUR POLE.

        · CHORUS ·

Candy Kitchen

By Lightnin' Sam Hopkins
& Jules Taub

CHILLY WINDS

2. I'M GOIN' WHERE THE COLD WON'T CHILL MY BONES, MY SWEET BABY,
    " " " " " " " " " BONES.
    WHEN I'M GONE TO MY LONG LONESOME HOME.

3. I'M GOIN' WHERE FOLKS ALL KNOW ME WELL, MY SWEET BABY,
    " " " " " " " " " " "
    WHEN I'M GONE TO MY LONG LONESOME HOME.

4. NOW, WHO WILL BE YOUR HONEY WHEN I'M GONE, MY SWEET BABY.
    " " " " " " " " " " " " "
    WHEN I'M GONE TO MY LONG LONESOME HOME.

CAN'T STOP LOVIN'

BY ELMORE JAMES
& J. TAUB

I CAN'T STOP LOV-IN'
I LOVED MY BA-BY
WHEN I LEAVE MY BA-BY
OH _____ BA-BY
OH _____ BA-BY

MY BA-BY TO-NIGHT
THIS MOR-NIN' SOON
SHE'S ALL A-LONE
COME AND WALK WITH ME
COME ALL A-LONE

I CAN'T STOP LOV-IN'
I LOVED MY BA-BY
WHEN I LEAVE MY BA-BY
OH BA-BY BA-BY
OH BA-BY BA-BY

MY BA-BY TO-NIGHT
THIS MORN-IN' SOON
SHE'S ALL A-LONE
COME AND WALK WITH ME
COME ALL A-LONE

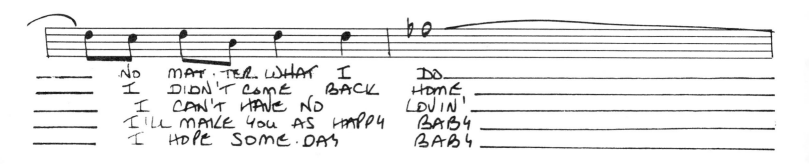

NO MAT·TER WHAT I   DO
I DIDN'T COME BACK   HOME
I CAN'T HAVE NO   LOVIN'
I'LL MAKE YOU AS HAPPY   BABY
I HOPE SOME·DAY   BABY

SHE WON'T TREAT ME   RIGHT.
'TIL THIS AFTER   NOON.
'CAUSE MY BABY'S   GONE.
AS ANY GIRL CAN   BE.
YOU WILL COME BACK   HOME.

MAKE A LITTLE LOVE

BY ELMORE JAMES
& J. TAUB

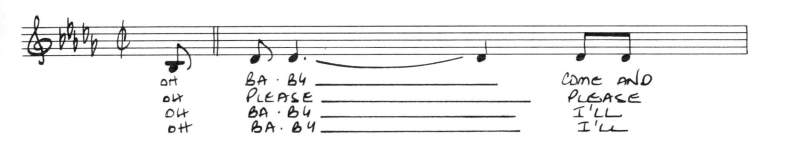

OH   BA·BY   COME AND
OH   PLEASE   PLEASE
OH   BA·BY   I'LL
OH   BA·BY   I'LL

48

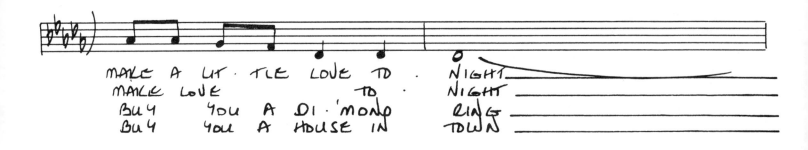

MAKE A LIT·TLE LOVE TO · NIGHT
MAKE LOVE TO · NIGHT
BUY YOU A DI ·'MOND RING
BUY YOU A HOUSE IN TOWN

OH BA·BY COME AND
OH PLEASE PLEASE
OH BA·BY I'LL
OH BA·BY I'LL

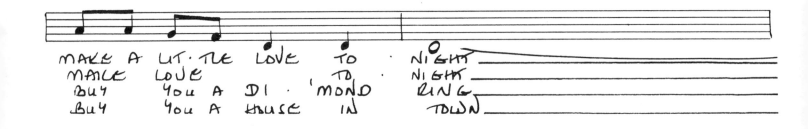

MAKE A LIT·TLE LOVE TO · NIGHT
MAKE LOVE TO · NIGHT
BUY YOU A DI ·'MOND RING
BUY YOU A HOUSE IN TOWN

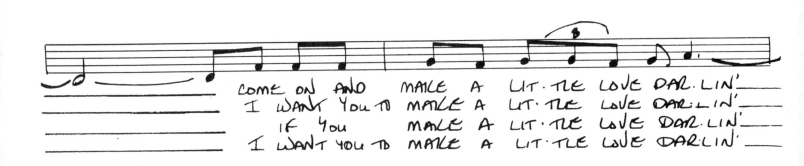

COME ON AND MAKE A LIT·TLE LOVE DAR·LIN'
I WANT YOU TO MAKE A LIT·TLE LOVE DAR·LIN'
IF YOU MAKE A LIT·TLE LOVE DAR·LIN'
I WANT YOU TO MAKE A LIT·TLE LOVE DAR·LIN'

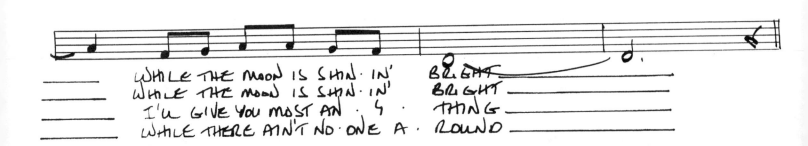

WHILE THE MOON IS SHIN·IN' BRIGHT
WHILE THE MOON IS SHIN·IN' BRIGHT
I'LL GIVE YOU MOST AN·Y·THING
WHILE THERE AIN'T NO·ONE A·ROUND

Corrina, Corrina

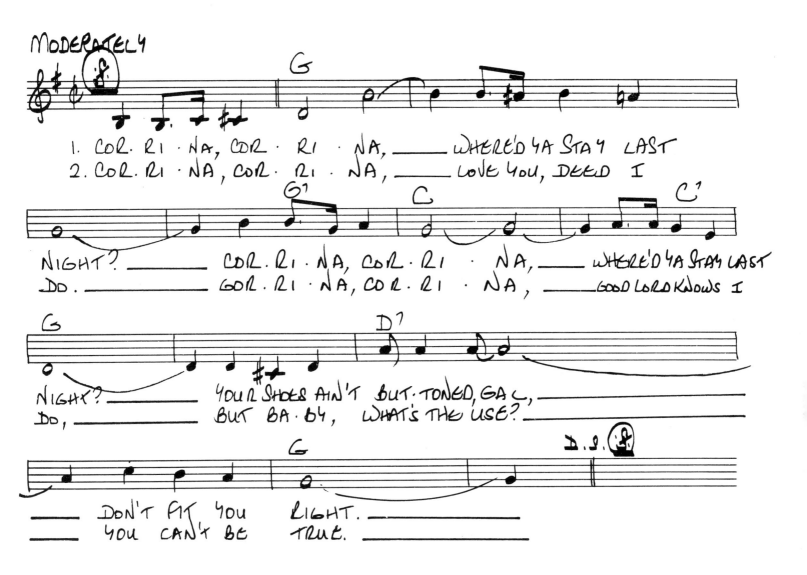

1. Cor·ri·na, cor·ri·na, _____ where'd ya stay last
2. Cor·ri·na, cor·ri·na, _____ love you, deed I

Night? _____ cor·ri·na, cor·ri·na, _____ where'd ya stay last
Do. _____ cor·ri·na, cor·ri·na, _____ good Lord knows I

Night? _____ your shoes ain't but·toned, gal, _____
Do, _____ but ba·by, what's the use? _____

_____ don't fit you right. _____
_____ you can't be true. _____

Darlin' You Know I Love You

BY B. B. KING AND
J. TAUB

(Slow, with Soul)

Now, dar-lin' you know I love you ____ and love you ____ by my-self; but you've gone and left me for some-bod-y else. ____ I think of you ev-'ry morn-in' ____ and dream of you ev-'ry night, and I would love to be with you al-

DELIA'S GONE
(ONE MORE ROUND)

(MODERATELY)

MISS DE·LIA, SHE TWO·TIMED HER TO·NY SAT·UR·DAY
HE BROUGHT HER A COCK·TAIL, THE VER·Y BEST___ IN THE
HE WANT·ED TO MAR·RY 'BUT SHE PRE·FERRED___ TO BE
SO TO·NY WAS LOCKED UP, THE JUDGE RE·FUSED___ TO SET
THEN TO·NY SAID "THANK YOU", "YOUR HON·OR TREAT·ED ME

NIGHT, AND ON THIS DATE, SHE MET HER FATE, HE SHOT HER DOWN AT
TOWN, BUT SHE RE·FUSED TO DOWN THE SHOT AND, SO HE SHOT HER
LOOSE, SHE DID NOT WANT A GOOSE TO COOK AND SO HE COOKED HER
BAIL. FOR SUCH A CRIME HE SHOULD DO TIME, SAY NINE·TY-NINE YEARS IN
FINE." HE KNEW THE JUDGE COULD WELL HAVE SAID: NINE HUN·DRED NINE·TY·

SIGHT.
DOWN. } DE·LIA'S GONE, ONE MORE ROUND, DE·LIA'S GONE!___ DE·LIA'S
GOOSE.
JAIL.
NINE.

GONE, ONE MORE ROUND, DE·LIA'S GONE!___ DE·LIA'S GONE, ONE MORE

ROUND, DE·LIA'S GONE!___ DE·LIA DID A "TWO TIME"..ON A SAT·UR·DAY

NIGHT, DE·LIA'S GONE, ONE MORE ROUND, DE·LIA'S GONE!___ SHE'S GONE!

D.S.

Don't Keep My Baby Long

BY LIGHTNIN' SAM HOPKINS
& JULES TAUB

DO YOU KNOW I TOOK THAT BOY I'VE TAKEN HIM FOR MY BEST
MAYBE I MAY HEAR FROM HER MAYBE I MAY HEAR FROM HER ONE
WELL I WOKE UP THIS MORNIN' JUST ABOUT THE BREAK OF

FRIEND _____ BUT HE
DAY _____ MAY. BE
DAY _____ I WENT

DONE TOOK MY LITTLE WOMAN YOU KNOW HE MUST BE AN ENEMY I DON'T
I MAY HEAR FROM HER MAYBE I MAY HEAR FROM HER ONE
TO GET SOME MILK ALL GONE A -

TRUST _____ YES IF HE
DAY _____ AND IF
WAY _____ OH LITTLE WOMAN

DON'T CARE IF MY LITTLE GIRL WAITS _____ PLEASE DON'T KEEP MY BABY
SHE DON'T FIND ME _____ BABY YOU DON'T DO WHAT YOU
HOPE YOU'LL COME BACK SOME DAY _____ AND WHEN YOU DO PLEASE CHANGE YOUR LOW

LONG _____
SAY _____
DOWN WAYS _____

Don't Start Cryin' Now

By James Moore
and Jerry West

MAN YOU GOT, BA-BY, HE DON'T MEAN YOU NO GOOD,
BRAG-GIN' 'BOUT YOUR WOMAN, — TAKE A LOOK AT MINE,

HE'S JUST WRECK-IN' YOUR NAME DOWN IN YOUR NEIGH-BOR-
— SHE'S SWEET AS ANY ANGEL; WANTS LOVIN' MOST ALL THE

HOOD. _____
TIME. _____

I Just Can't Leave You

BY JAMES MOORE

(SLOWLY)

(1.) I JUST CAN'T LEAVE YOU, DAR-LIN', — THIS I FIND SO HARD TO
(2.) — GOD — KNOWS I LOVE YOU, — THIS IS ALL I HAVE TO

DO, _____   I JUST CAN'T LEAVE YOU, DAR-LIN', —
SAY, _____   — GOD — KNOWS I LOVE YOU, —

THIS I FIND SO HARD TO   DO, _____   GOD KNOWS I
THIS IS ALL I HAVE TO   SAY, _____   YOU DRIVE ME

TRIED, BUT I JUST CAN'T GET A·LONG WITH YOU. _____ (2.) WHEN I FIRST
CRAZY. ONE DAY I'LL· BE ____ ON MY WAY. _____

MET YOU DAR·LIN' ____ YOU WERE SO NICE AND SWEET TO ME, _____

____ WHEN I FIRST MET YOU, BA·BY, ____ YOU WERE SO NICE AND SWEET TO

ME; _____ NOW IT'S GOT SO BAD

I'M A·SHAMED TO BE SEEN WITH YOU IN THE STREET. _____

Down And Out Blues

1. SAYS I AIN'T GOT NO AIR-PLANE, AIN'T GOT NO AU-TO-MO-BILE, — I AIN'T GOT NO MON-EY, GUESS I'LL HAVE TO ROB AND STEAL. FOR WHEN I WAKE UP IN THE MORN-IN' I CAN'T EAT A DE-CENT MEAL, I HAD BAD LUCK IN MY FAM-I-LY, — I GUESS YOU KNOW JUST HOW I FEEL.

2. WHEN I HAD PLENTY OF MONEY,
AND PLENTY OF CLOTHES,
THESE CHICAGO WOMEN
FOLLOWED ME IN DROVES.
· CHORUS ·

3. SAYS, I ASKED MY MAMA,
TO TAKE ME BACK ONE MO',
SHE SAID, "YOU AIN'T GOT NO
MONEY,
SWEET PAPA THERE'S THE DO'."
· CHORUS ·

4. NOW MY WOMEN STANDIN' ON THE CORNER,
WITH THEIR WEEKLY PAY,
IF THEY THINK I WANT TO BORROW SOMETHIN'
THEY TURN AND GO ANOTHER WAY.
· CHORUS ·

5. WHEN I MAKE THIS PAYDAY,
GET MY MONEY IN MY HAND,
YOU WOMEN NEEDN'T COME A-RUNNIN'
YOU CAN FIND YOU ANOTHER MAN.
· CHORUS ·

EARLY IN THE MORNING

BY ELMORE JAMES
& JOE JOSEA

WELL IT'S EAR-LY IN THE MORN-ING
WELL I GOT TO LEAVE MY BA-BY
SHE CAN GET SO SEN-TI-MEN-TAL

AND MY BA-BY CAN'T BE FOUND
'CAUSE SHE GIVES ME SUCH A THRILL
WHEN THE LIGHTS ARE WAY DOWN LOW

WELL IT'S EAR-LY IN THE MORN-ING
WELL I GOT TO LEAVE MY BA-BY
SHE CAN GET SO SEN-TI-MEN-TAL

AND MY BA-BY CAN'T BE FOUND
'CAUSE SHE GIVES ME SUCH A THRILL
WHEN THE LIGHTS ARE WAY DOWN LOW

I'M GON-NA PACK UP AND LEAVE HER
WELL SHE TAKES ME BACK IN THE MORN-IN'
THE WAY THAT GAL CAN THRILL ME

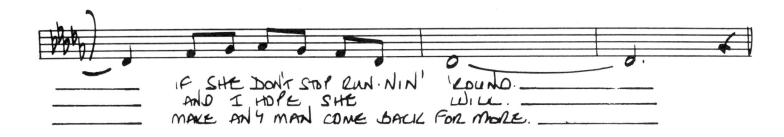

IF SHE DON'T STOP RUN-NIN' 'ROUND. _____
AND I HOPE SHE WILL. _____
MAKE ANY MAN COME BACK FOR MORE. _____

LATE HOURS AT MIDNIGHT

BY ELMORE JAMES
& JOE JOSEA

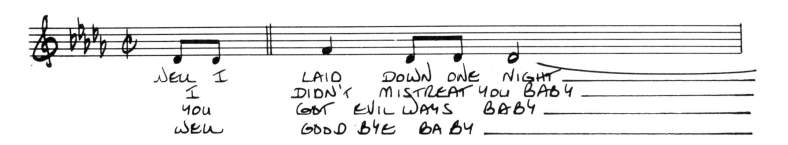

WELL I LAID DOWN ONE NIGHT _____
I DIDN'T MISTREAT YOU BABY _____
YOU GOT EVIL WAYS BABY _____
WELL GOODBYE BABY _____

60

Empty Mailbox Blues

2. WHEN I LOOKED OUT THIS MORNIN', THE MAILMAN PASSED ON BY,
   " " " " " " " " GOT THE EMPTY MAILBOX BLUES, AND I FEEL SO BAD I COULD DIE.

3. ON LAST SATURDAY MORNIN' YOU TOOK THE NUMBER TWELVE TRAIN,
   " " " " " " " " NOW I MISS YOU SO MUCH, BABY, I WISH YOU WERE BACK AGAIN.

4. SINCE YOU PACKED UP YOUR SUITCASE AND WAVED GOODBYE TO ME,
   " " " " " " " " EV'RY DAY SEEMS LIKE A YEAR AND EACH NIGHT IS LIKE TWO OR THREE.

5. WISH YOU'D WRITE ME SOON, HONEY, I WORRY OVER YOU,
   " " " " " " " " IF I HAD A LETTER FROM YOU, I KNOW THAT I WOULDN'T BE SO BLUE.

Fishing Blues

WENT UP ON THE HILL 'BOUT TWELVE O'CLOCK, — REACHED RIGHT BACK AND
LOOKED DOWN THE RIVER ABOUT ONE O'CLOCK, — _____
PUT ON THE SKILLET, _____

GOT ME A POLE, — WENT TO THE HARD WARE, GOT ME A HOOK, —
I GOT SO HUNGRY DIDN'T KNOW WHAT TO DO, — _____
PUT ON THE LID _____

PUT THAT LINE RIGHT ON THAT HOOK. SAY, YOU'VE BEEN A FISH IN'
I'M GONNA GET ME A CAT FISH TOO.
MAMA'S GONNA COOK A LITTLE SHORTNING BREAD.

ALL THE TIME, — I'M A GO IN' FISH IN' TOO. I

BET YOUR LIFE, YOUR LOV IN' WIFE, I'LL CATCH MORE FISH THAN

YOU. AN' 4 FISH BIT IN' — GOT YOUR BAIT,

HERE'S A LIT-TLE SOME-THIN' I WOULD LIKE TO RE-LATE, ___

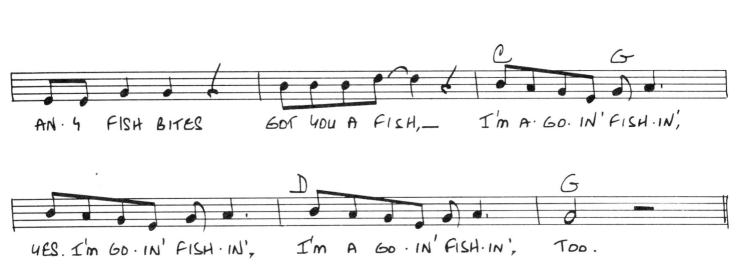

AN-Y FISH BITES GOT YOU A FISH,___ I'M A-GO-IN' FISH-IN',

YES, I'M GO-IN' FISH-IN', I'M A GO-IN' FISH-IN', TOO.

GEORGIA STOCKADE

(LIVELY)

WAY DOWN ___ IN CO-LUM-BUS, GEOR-
NIGHT ___ AS ___ I LAY SLEEP-
GO, ___ IT ___ SEEMS A LONG

GIA, ___ THAT'S WHERE I DON'T WANT TO BE. ___
IN', ___ I DREAMT I HELD YOU IN MY ARMS. ___
TIME, ___ THAT'S WHEN I WAS FREE AND ON MY OWN. ___

Found My Baby Crying

By Lightnin' Sam Hopkins & Stan Lewis

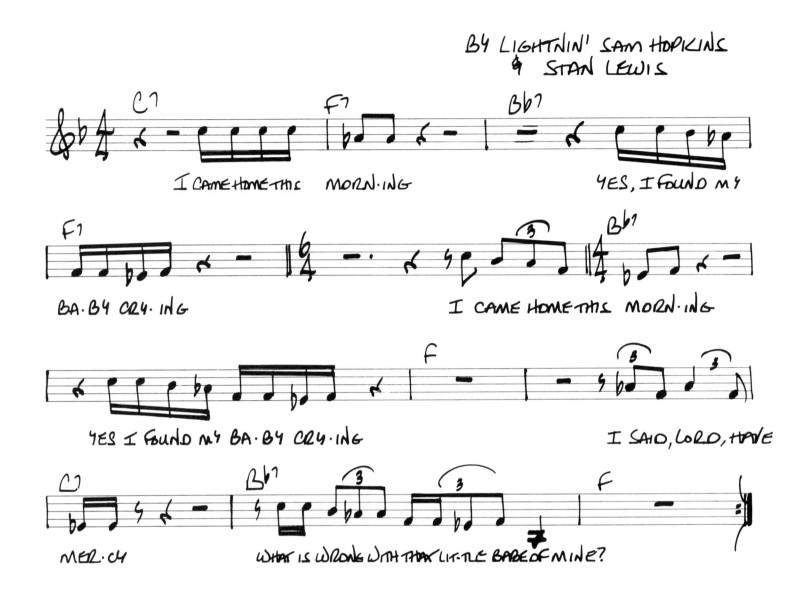

I came home this morn-ing   Yes, I found my

ba-by cry-ing   I came home this morn-ing

yes I found my ba-by cry-ing   I said, Lord, have

mer-cy   what is wrong with that lit-tle babe of mine?

2. You know it hurt me so bad, see those tears roll down my cheeks
   You know it hurt me so bad, see those tears roll down my cheeks
   You know I didn't have no money, old Lightnin' didn't have a bite to eat.

3. Don't cry, baby, you know things are bound to change
   Don't cry, baby, you know things are bound to change
   If I didn't bring the bacon in winter, records show old Lightnin'
   will bring it in the spring.

Gambler's Blues

By Lightnin' Sam Hopkins
& Stan Lewis

2) You know I lost all my money, in her no good gambling game
I lost all my money, for I didn't know a good gambler's game
I was on my bad luck _ kept gambling just the same.

3) Man when you lose that no good money, sit around with your head hung down
When you lose that no good money, sit around with your head hung down
Wake up the next morning happy, I am the best gambler in this town.

Got The Lonesome Blues

MODERATELY

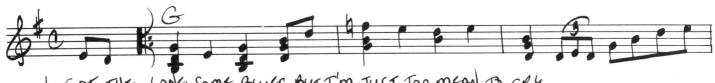

1. GOT THE LONE-SOME BLUES, BUT I'M JUST TOO MEAN TO CRY,

GOT THE LONE-SOME BLUES, BUT I'M JUST TOO MEAN TO

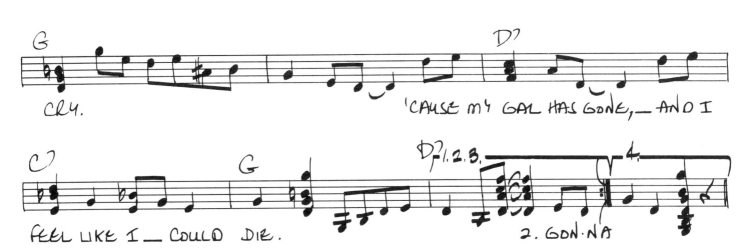

CRY. 'CAUSE MY GAL HAS GONE,— AND I

FEEL LIKE I — COULD DIE.

2. GON·NA

2. GONNA LEAVE THIS PLACE, GONNA LEAVE THIS LONESOME TOWN,
    " TRY " TO " FIND " SOMEWHERE " THAT " THEY " AIN'T " NO " BLUES " AROUN'.
3. GRAB A RAILROAD TRAIN, GOIN' FAR AWAY TONIGHT,
    I WON'T FEEL SO BAD WHEN I SEE THAT MORNIN' LIGHT.
4. FIND ANOTHER GAL, FIND A GAL TO LOVE ME TRUE,
    " WON'T " BE " LONESOME " THEN, " AND " I " WON'T " NO " MO' " BE BLUE.

Hand in Hand

BY ELMORE JAMES
& JOE JOSEA

HIGH-PRICE BLUES

I'll tell you some-thing, ain't no joke,

High cost of liv-in' is keep-in' me broke. Pri-ces go-in' high-er,

'way up high-er, pri-ces go-in' so high, what

more can we do?

WALKED IN A MEAT MARKET JUST ABOUT NOON,
HEAR THEM HOLLERIN', "NOW THE COW JUMPED OVER THE MOON."
· CHORUS ·
JOHNNY'S GONE TO WAR, JOHNNY'S GONE TO SEA,
BUT I TELL YOU HIGH PRICES IS KILLIN' ME.
· CHORUS ·
MEAT, BUTTER, AND EGGS GETTIN' HIGHER STILL,
YOU DON'T EVEN GET NO CHANGE OUT OF A FIVE-DOLLAR BILL.
· CHORUS ·
PRICES GOIN' HIGHER, YES, 'WAY UP HIGHER,
WELL, IT'S NO DISGRACE TO BE POOR, BUT IT'S A LITTLE UNHANDY FOR ME
· CHORUS ·
THE HORSES AND THE NUMBERS — ODDS ARE STILL THE SAME,
LOOKS LIKE THE PRICES WOULD RAISE TEN PER CENT ON THE GAME.
· CHORUS ·
PRICES GOIN' HIGHER, YES, 'WAY UP HIGHER.
PRICES GOIN' SO HIGH, I DON'T THINK I WILL WORK NO MORE.

HOUSE UPON THE HILL

BY LIGHTNIN' SAM HOPKINS

I WANT YOU TO COME ON AND GO WITH ME BA·BY TO THAT BIG HOUSE

I GOT BUILT ON THE HILL   I GOT GOOD VEG·TBLES THERE

DAR·LIN' KNOW IT'S GOIN' GIVE YOUR A HEART A THRILL I WANT YOU COME ON AND GO

TO THAT LIT TLE HOUSE I GOT BUILT UPON THE HILL

YES YOU KNOW I   GOT SO MUCH VEGTA·BLES THERE

THEY'S GOIN' GIVE YOUR LITTLE HEART A THRILL

How Can You Keep On Movin'

HOW CAN YOU KEEP ON MOV-IN' UN-LESS YOU MI-GRATE TOO? THEY TELL YOU TO KEEP ON MOV-IN', BUT MI-GRATE YOU MUST NOT DO, THE ON-LY REA-SON FOR MOV-IN', AND THE REA-SON WHY I ROAM, IS TO MOVE TO A NEW LO-CA-TION, AND FIND MY-SELF A HOME. ____ 2. I TOO. _____

I CAN'T GO BACK TO THE HOMESTEAD,
  THE SHACK NO LONGER STANDS
THEY SAID I WASN'T NEEDED,
  HAD NO CLAIM TO THE LAND
THEY SAID "COME ON, GET MOVIN', IT'S THE ONLY THING FOR YOU"
BUT HOW CAN YOU GET MOVIN' UNLESS YOU MIGRATE TOO.

I Believe

BY J. TAUB

I Held My Baby Last Night

BY ELMORE JAMES

I HELD MY BA-BY LAST NIGHT
AND THOUGHT EV'RY-THING WAS ALL RIGHT
I HELD MY BA-BY LAST NIGHT
AND THOUGHT EV'RY-THING WAS ALL RIGHT
SHE WOKE UP EAR-LY IN THE MOR-NING
ALL SHE WANT TO DO WAS FUSS AND FIGHT.

I Don't Believe She'd Know Me

I don't be·lieve my ba·by'd know me, ___

You know I been gone ___ so long. ___ I

won·der would she know me ___ if I'd ease in·to my

hap·py home. ___ "I won·der would my ba·by know me," is the

word I heard her say, ___ "the last time I seen you, Lord, you was

goin' a·way." ___ Now won·der would she know me, ___

I BEEN GONE _____ SO LONG. _____

_____ AND I WAIT AND I WOR-RY, SERV-IN'

TIME _____ ON THIS FARM. _____

ONE DAY MY BABY TOLD ME ___ TOLD ME NOT TO LEAVE.
I WALKED OUT THE DOOR, TURNED MY BACK AT THE BREEZE.
AND·A SHE TOLD ME NOT TO LEAVE·HER, THIS IS THE REASON WHY,
SAID, "IF YOU GO ON THE RIVER YOU MIGHT MAKE IT TO THE
OTHER SIDE."

THAT'S WHY I WONDER WOULD SHE KNOW ME,
I BEEN GONE SO LONG,
SINGIN' THESE OLD BLUES ALL ABOUT MY LONESOME HOME.

I Was A Fool

BY ELMORE JAMES
& J. TAUB

MAY NEV·ER SEE YOU ANY·MORE   WELL, AL·

WAYS LOVE YOU DAR·LIN'___   HOUND YOU EV·'RY WHERE YOU

GO   WOH ___ BYE ___

GOOD·BYE BA·BY ___   YES, GOOD·BYE

BA·BY ___   YES GOOD·BYE BYE BA·BY ___

WOH ___ BYE BA·BY ___

YEA, BA·BY GOOD·BYE ___

I'm a Stranger Here

AIN'T IT HARD TO STUM·BLE   WHEN YOU'VE GOT NO PLACE_TO

FALL?   AIN'T IT HARD TO STUM·BLE_WHEN YOU'VE GOT_NO PLACE_TO_

FALL?   IN THIS WHOLE WIDE_ WORLD _ I'VE GOT NO PLACE_ AT

ALL.   I'M A STRAN·GER HERE. I'M A STRAN·GER EV·'RY. WHERE.

_   I WOULD GO HOME BUT. HON·EY, I'M A STRAN·GER THERE. _

HITCH UP MY BUGGY, SADDLE UP MY BLACK MARE. (2x)
GOIN' TO FIND ME A FAIR DEAL IN THIS WORLD SOMEWHERE. (CHORUS)

I'M WORRIED NOW BUT I WON'T BE WORRIED LONG. (2X)
IT TAKES A WORRIED MAN TO SING A WORRIED SONG. (CHORUS)

BABY CAUGHT THE KATY, SHE LEFT ME A MULE TO RIDE. (2x)
WHEN THE TRAIN PULLED OUT THAT MULE LAID DOWN AND DIED. (CHORUS)

LOOKED DOWN THE TRACK JUST AS FAR AS I COULD SEE. (2x)
AND A LITTLE BITTY HAND KEPT A·WAVIN' BACK AT ME. (CHORUS)

I'm a King Bee

By James Moore

WELL, I'M A KING BEE, BUT I'VE BEEN A·ROUND YOUR
(WELL, I'M A) KING BEE, WANT YOU TO BE MY

HIVE, WELL, I'M A KING BEE,
QUEEN, WELL, I'M A KING BEE,

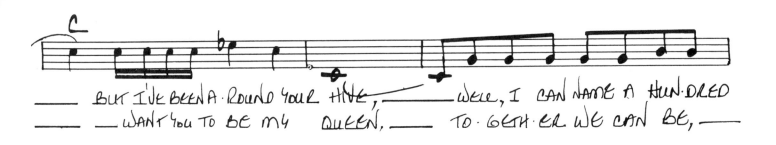

BUT I'VE BEEN A·ROUND YOUR HIVE, WELL, I CAN NAME A HUN·DRED
WANT YOU TO BE MY QUEEN, TO·GETH·ER WE CAN BE,

REA·SONS TO LET ME COME IN·SIDE.
HON·EY. FOR·EV·ER AND EV·ER SEEN.

I'm Comin' Home

BY LIGHTNIN' SAM HOPKINS

I'm com-in' home ba-by

Darlin' I ain't doin' no good out here

I'm com-in' home now dar-lin'

I ain't doin' no good out here

I know it don't make you much dif-fer-ence

But I want you to feel I care.

2) You didn't tell me to leave
Baby I just left on my own
You didn't tell me to leave
Little girl, I just left on my own
That's the reason I want you to make me welcome
Look out! I'm comin' home.

3) Did you get my letter
Tellin' you I'd be home before long?
Did you get my letter
Tellin' you I'd be home before long?
But it don't make no difference if you didn't get it
Look out! Old Lightnin's comin' home.

I'm Gonna Ride That Southern Railroad Line

2. I'M GOIN' WHERE THE CHILLY WIND DON'T BLOW, (2x)
   I'M GONNA RIDE THAT SOUTHERN RAILWAY LINE.

3. I'M GOIN' WHERE THE SUNSHINE FEELS GOOD, (2x)
   I'M GONNA RIDE THAT SOUTHERN RAILWAY LINE.

4. I'M GOIN' WHERE THE FOLKS DON'T SHOVEL SNOW, (2x)
   I'M GONNA RIDE THAT SOUTHERN RAILWAY LINE.

5. I'M GOIN' WHERE THE FOLKS ALL KNOW MY NAME, (2x)
   I'M GONNA RIDE THAT SOUTHERN RAILWAY LINE.

6. I'LL NEVER COME BACK HERE WHERE I BEEN BLUE, (2x)
   I'M GONNA RIDE THAT SOUTHERN RAILWAY LINE.

I'm Gonna Keep What I've Got

By James Moore

HEY, LIT-TLE GIRL, _____ YOU'RE LOOK-IN' GOOD TO ME;

YOU MOVE ME, BA-BY,

LIKE A SUR-GEON MOVES A TREE,

DON'T WANT TO GET MY-SELF IN NO SPOT,

DON'T WANT TO START SOME THING I CAN'T STOP, SO I'LL BE LEAV-IN';

I'M GON-NA KEEP WHAT I'VE GOT. (2.) YOU LOVE YOUR

MAN _____ WITH A WHOLE LOT OF SOUL,

EV-'RY- THING SHINES, IT CAN'T BE SOL-ID

GOLD BUT IF YOU PLAY WITH FIRE___ YOU'RE
GON·NA GET BURNED, IF YOU DON'T BE·LIEVE ME TRY IT
OUT ON YOUR LINE WHILE IT'S HOT
I'D BET·TER KEEP WHAT I'VE GOT___

I'VE GOT TO BE WITH YOU TONIGHT

BY JAMES MOORE

I'VE GOT TO BE WITH YOU TO·NIGHT,___
TO·MOR·ROW I KNOW THAT YOU'LL BE GONE,___
I'LL BE HURT·IN' FOR MY BA·BY,
WHAT CAN I·DO WITH THESE EMP·TY ARMS,___

I'm So Sorry

BY JAMES MOORE

(SLOW)

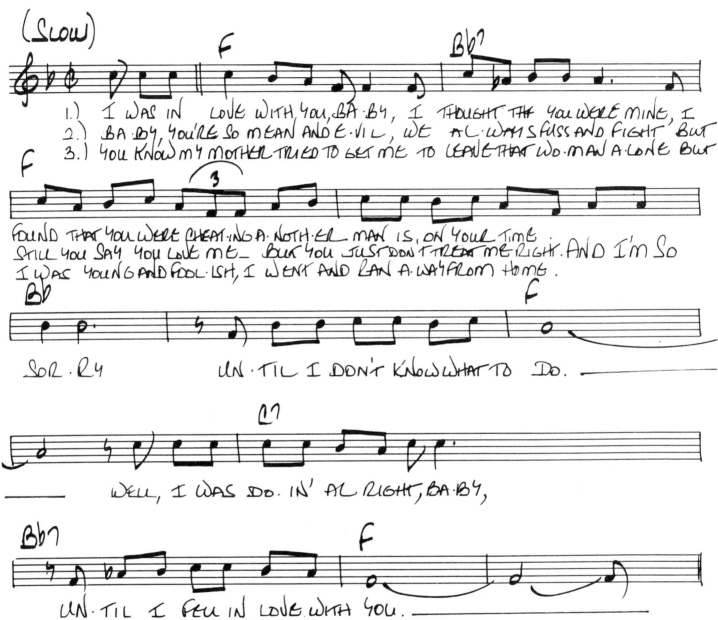

1.) I WAS IN LOVE WITH YOU, BA-BY, I THOUGHT THAT YOU WERE MINE, I
2.) BA-BY, YOU'RE SO MEAN AND E-VIL, WE AL-WAYS FUSS AND FIGHT, BUT
3.) YOU KNOW MY MOTHER TRIED TO GET ME TO LEAVE THAT WO-MAN A-LONE BUT

FOUND THAT YOU WERE CHEAT-ING A-NOTH-ER MAN IS, ON YOUR TIME
STILL YOU SAY YOU LOVE ME_ BUT YOU JUST DON'T TREAT ME RIGHT. AND I'M SO
I WAS YOUNG AND FOOL-ISH, I WENT AND RAN A-WAY FROM HOME.

SOR-RY UN-TIL I DON'T KNOW WHAT TO DO. _

_ WELL, I WAS DO-IN' AL-RIGHT, BA-BY,

UN-TIL I FELL IN LOVE WITH YOU. _

I'm Tired of Trouble

By Lightnin' Sam Hopkins

TRY-IN' TO SELL MY TROU-BLES

TROU-BLES I'VE HAD ALL MY DAYS

TRY-IN' TO SELL MY TROU-BLES

TROU-BLES I'VE HAD ALL MY DAYS

SOME-TIMES I FEEL MY TROU-BLES WITH THE WO-MEN

GON-NA TAKE OLE LIGHT-NIN' TO HIS GRAVE

2) I TOLD MY MAMA I WAS IN TROUBLE — SOMETHING I DIDN'T
   WANT HER TO KNOW
   I TOLD MY MAMA I WAS IN TROUBLE — SOMETHING I DIDN'T
   WANT HER TO KNOW
   MAMA SAID: "SON, YOU'RE HOME NOW — I'LL PRAY THERE
   AIN'T GONNA BE TROUBLES NO MO'."

I'm Your Hoochie Coochie Man

BY WILLIE DIXON

I'm Your Bread Maker, Baby

By James Moore

1.) Well, I'm your bread maker, baby __ and you can roll my
2.) You got me feelin' so good, __ just like I knew you

dough; Yes, you can work for me, baby, __
would. Well, I am stuck on __ you __

you're gonna want some more, come on and work with me,
just like __ glue sticks to wood. I'm gonna love you, __

baby, __ You're gonna want some more. __
baby, __ Because I knew I could. __

2.) I'm gonna work all __ day I'm gonna work all

night, ain't gonna stop workin', baby,

NOT TILL MY WORK IS DONE. YOU GON-NA BE WITH ME,

BA-BY. UN-TIL MORN-ING COMES.——

DYNAMITE

BY JAMES MOORE

1.) WELL, I'M DY-NA-MITE, BA-BY, ALL YOU DO IS LIGHT MY
2.) WELL, I'LL BE YOUR HAN-DY-MAN! AND I'LL WORK FROM SUN TO
3.) WELL, I'M DY-NA-MITE, BA-BY, I NEED YOU TO LIGHT MY

FUSE! WELL, I'M DY-NA-MITE, BA-BY, ALL YOU DO IS LIGHT MY
SUN. WELL, I'LL BE YOUR HAN-DY-MAN AND I'LL WORK FROM SUN TO
FUSE. WELL, I'M DY-NA-MITE, BA-BY, I NEED YOU TO LIGHT MY

FUSE! WELL, WITH MY EYE'S CLOSED, BA-BY,
SUN. WELL I'— AIN'T GONNA LEAVE MY JOB, BABY,
FUSE! WELL, WHEN THE LIGHTS ARE LOW,

I'M GONNA BLOW A-WAY YOUR BLUES!
UN-TIL I'M SURE MY WORK IS DONE!
I'M GON-NA BLOW A-WAY YOUR BLUES!

I've Been Your Good Thing

By James Moore

FRIENDS___ THINK I'M A DEV·IL AND, BA·BY,

YOU ARE AN IN·NO·CENT SAINT BUT,

BA·BY, I KNOW DIFF.'RENT, OH

DAR·LIN' I KNOW YOU AIN'T. (D.C. AL FINE)

MAILBOX BLUES

BY JAMES MOORE
AND REGINALD STUART

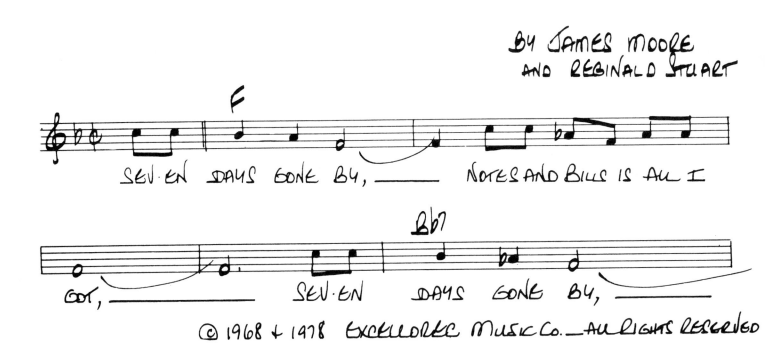

SEV·EN DAYS GONE BY, ___ NOTES AND BILLS IS ALL I

GOT, ___ SEV·EN DAYS GONE BY, ___

94

Jake Head Boogie

By Lightnin' Sam Hopkins
& Jules Taub

WE GOT DRUNK LAST NIGHT MAN YES AND THE NIGHT BE.
I DON'T WANT NO DIXIE WOMAN TALKIN' 'BOUT MAN IN MY
THIS TIME NOW BA·BY JUST GOT TO LET YOU

FORE _____
FACE _____
GO _____

WE GOT
I DON'T
THIS

DRUNK LAST NIGHT MAN YES AND THE NIGHT BE.
WANT NO DIXIE WOMAN TALKIN' 'BOUT MAN IN MY
TIME NOW BA·BY JUST GOT TO LET YOU

FORE _____
FACE _____
GO _____

COME
THERE'S A
COME

HOME TEL·LIN' ME YES GONNA GET DRUNK COME
WHOLE LOT OF WOM·EN JUST RARIN' TO TAKE HER
HOME TELLIN' ME THAT YOU WON'T GET DRUNK NO

MORE. _____
PLACE. _____
MORE. _____

Jim Crow Blues

Slow Blues

I'm TIRED ___ of BE-ING JIM ___ CROWED,

GON-NA LEAVE ___ THIS JIM CROW TOWN ___

DOG-GON MY BLACK SOUL, I'M SWEET CHI-CA-GO BOUND ___

___ YES SIR, I'M LEAV-ING HERE ___ FROM THIS OLD JIM CROW TOWN.

1.2.3.4. 5.

2. (YES, I'm)

2. YES, I'M GOING UP NORTH WHERE THEY TELL ME MONEY GROWS ON TREES.
I DON'T GIVE A GODDAM EVEN IF MY SOUL WILL FREEZE.
I'M GOING WHERE I'LL NEED MY WOOLEN SLEEVES.

3. I GOT MY HAT, GOT MY OVERCOAT, DON'T NEED NOTHIN' BUT SHOES.
THESE OLD LOAFERS GONNA WALK AWAY MY BLUES
WHEN MY GIRL HEARS ABOUT THAT SHE'S GONNA BE BAD NEWS.

4. I'M GOING UP NORTH, BABY, I CAN'T CARRY YOU,
AIN'T A THING IN THAT COUNTRY A GIRL LIKE YOU CAN DO,
I'M GONNA GET ME A NEW LOVE, BABY, 'CAUSE, I'M THROUGH WITH YOU.

5. GONNA TELL THE BIG BOSS OFF, GIVE HIM A PIECE OF MY MIND
FROM NOW ON LITTLE BABY, I'LL BE HARD TO FIND
GOIN' TO CHICAGO, GONNA LEAVE THE SOUTH, LEAVE IT ALL FAR BEHIND.

JODY MAN

By James Moore

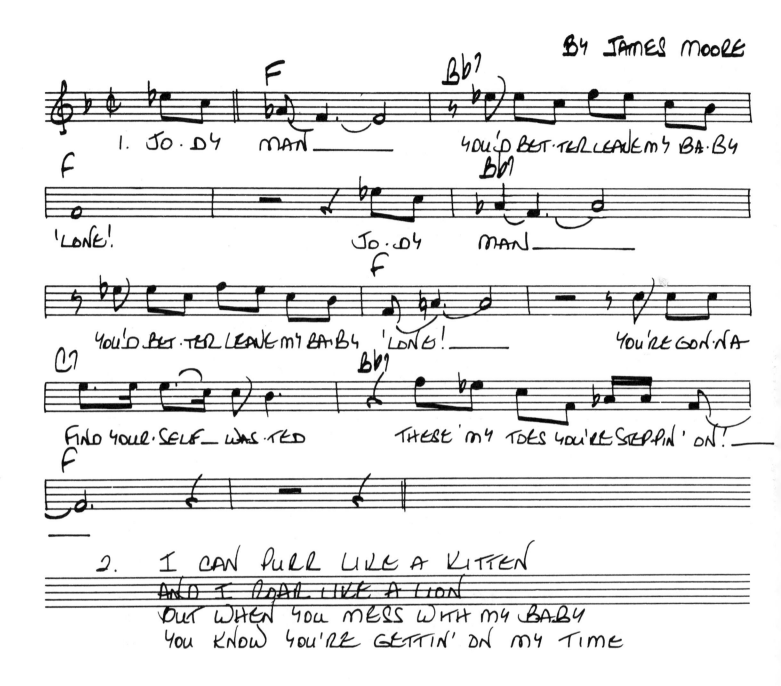

1. JO·DY MAN _____ YOU'D BET·TER LEAVE MY BA·BY 'LONE! JO·DY MAN _____ YOU'D BET·TER LEAVE MY BA·BY 'LONE! _____ YOU'RE GON·NA FIND YOUR·SELF_ WAS·TED THESE MY TOES YOU'RE STEP·PIN' ON! _____

2. I CAN PURR LIKE A KITTEN
~~AND I ROAR LIKE A LION~~
BUT WHEN YOU MESS WITH MY BABY
YOU KNOW YOU'RE GETTIN' ON MY TIME

JOE TURNER

LAST WEEK OLD JOE TUR·NER CAME TO TOWN,

LAST WEEK OLD JOE TUR·NER CAME TO TOWN.

JOE TUR·NER ___ GOT MY MAN AND GONE.

2.(MY) CALL.

2. MY MAN IS IN NASHVILLE, STUCK IN JAIL, (2x)
AND I CAN'T EVEN RAISE HIS BAIL.

3. MY MAN GOT HIMSELF INTO A FIGHT, (2x)
HE STABBED A MAN ON MONDAY NIGHT.

4. ON TUESDAY HE CAME TO ME TO HIDE,(2x)
SO I SAID, "HON,' COME ON INSIDE."

5. JOE TURNER FOUND OUT WHAT MY MAN DONE, (2x)
JOE TURNER GOT MY MAN AND GONE.

6. WHEN I'LL SEE MY MAN NO ONE CAN TELL, (2x)
JOE TURNER'S LOCKED HIM IN A CELL.

Kansas City Blues

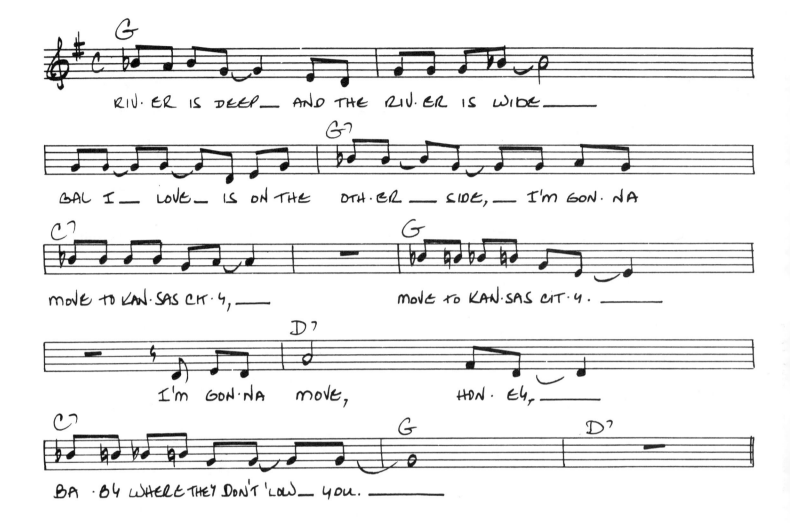

RIV·ER IS DEEP__ AND THE RIV·ER IS WIDE____

GAL I__ LOVE__ IS ON THE OTH·ER__ SIDE,__ I'M GON·NA

MOVE TO KAN·SAS CIT·Y, __ MOVE TO KAN·SAS CIT·Y. ____

I'M GON·NA MOVE, HON·EY, ____

BA·BY WHERE THEY DON'T 'LOW__ YOU. ____

2. IF I WAS A CATFISH SWIMMIN' IN THE SEA,
ALL THEM PRETTY GALS WOULD COME SWIMMIN' AFTER ME.
GONNA MOVE TO KANSAS CITY, MOVE TO KANSAS CITY,
GONNA MOVE, HONEY, BABY WHERE THEY DON'T 'LOW YOU.

3. IF YOU DON'T LIKE MY PEACHES DON'T SHAKE MY TREE,
I LIKE MY WOMAN, SHE SURE LIKES ME,
WE'RE GONNA MOVE TO KANSAS CITY, MOVE TO KANSAS
GONNA MOVE HONEY, BABY WHERE THEY DON'T 'LOW YOU.

LAST AFFAIR

BY LIGHTNIN' SAM HOPKINS & JULES TAUB

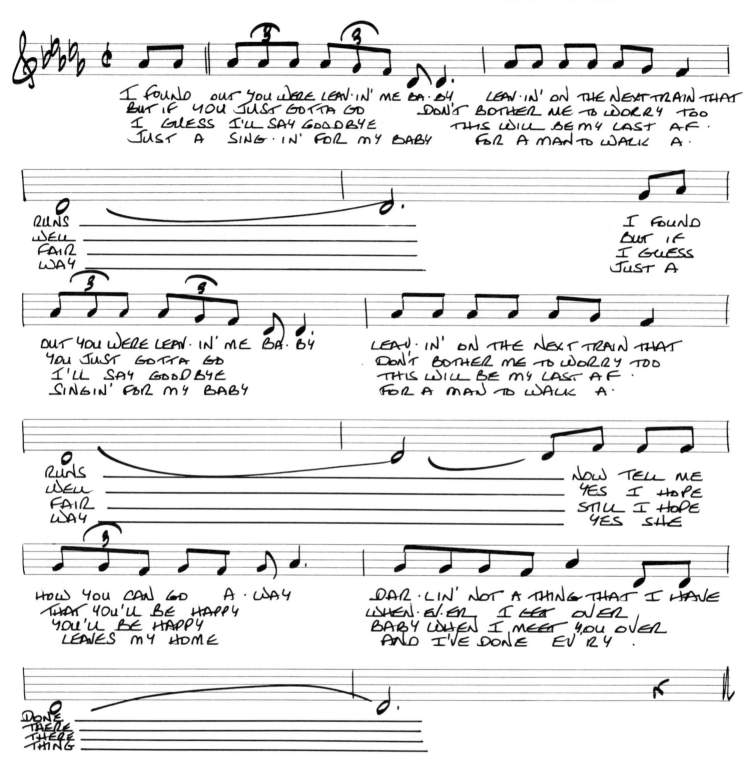

Lonesome Blues

I woke up this mornin', feel-in' sad and blue,
ba-by done quit me. What am I gon-na do?__ You know I'm
lone-some.__ And the blues is in my way._____ I may be
down and out to-day. But I'll__ be up some-day._____ __

Boys, ain't it hard lovin' another man's girlfriend?
Can't see her when you want to, got to see her when you can.
· Chorus ·
I got to walk by myself, sleep by myself,
while the woman I love she's lovin' somebody else.
· Chorus ·
My baby left me, she left me broken down,
said "Goodbye, daddy, I'll meet you in another town."
· Chorus ·
I wake up in the morning, 'bout the break of day,
reach against the pillow where my baby used to lay.
· Chorus ·

Lonesome Dog Blues

By Lightnin' Sam Hopkins

I GOT A DOG IN MY BACK YARD _____ HOWLED _____ THE
YOU KNOW A THING'S SO SAD _____ WHEN _____ A

DAY MY BA·BY'S GONE _____ I GOT A
DOG FEELS IT DEEP DOWN IN HIS HEART _____ YOU KNOW

DOG IN MY BACK YARD _____ HOWLED _____ THE
A THINGS SO SAD _____ WHEN _____ A

DAY MY BA·BY'S GONE _____ YES HE
DOG FEELS IT DEEP DOWN IN HIS HEART _____ GUESS YOU

PUTS MY MIND ON A WON·DER _____ HOW THAT THING WAS GO·IN' A·
KNOW A MAN CAN'T HELP BUT MESS AROUND HER WHEN A DOG IN HIS BACK YARD

LONG _____
HATES TO SEE THEM PART. _____

LONESOME ROAD

(SLOWLY)

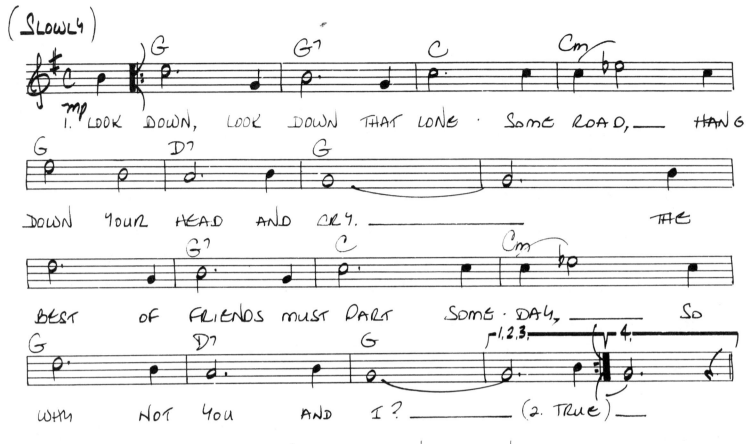

1. LOOK DOWN, LOOK DOWN THAT LONE · SOME ROAD,___ HANG DOWN YOUR HEAD AND CRY. _____ THE BEST OF FRIENDS MUST PART SOME · DAY, ___ SO WHY NOT YOU AND I? _____ (2. TRUE)___

2. TRUE LOVE, TRUE LOVE, WHAT HAVE I DONE,
   THAT MAKES YOU WANT TO PART?
   YOU'VE TAKEN ALL THE LOVE I HAVE,
   AND NOW YOU BREAK MY HEART.

3. SOMETIMES I WISH THAT I HAD DIED,
   HAD DIED 'FORE I WAS BORN;
   BEFORE I SAW YOUR SMILIN' FACE,
   AND HEARD YOUR LYIN' TONGUE.

4. I'LL TRAVEL DOWN THAT LONESOME ROAD,
   AND NEVER HAVE A HOME.
   I WANT NO OTHER LOVE BUT YOU,
   AND SO I'LL WALK ALONE.

LONG·HANDLED SHOVEL

(MODERATELY)

1. IT TAKES A LONG HAN·DLED SHOV·EL TO DIG A SIX·FOOT HOLE. _____

_____ IT TAKES A LONG HAN·DLED SHOV·EL TO DIG A SIX · FOOT

HOLE. _____ IT TAKES A LONG LEG·GED WO·MAN TO

MAKE ME LOSE MY SOUL. _____ 2. IT TAKES A _____

2. IT TAKES A FAST·MOVIN' WOMAN TO MAKE ME SATISFIED.
   BUT THEN A FAST·TALKIN' WOMAN WILL DRIVE ME RIGHT OUTSIDE.

3. IT TAKES A BIG·HEARTED WOMAN TO MAKE A MAN FEEL GLAD.
   BUT THEN A SHORT·TEMPERED WOMAN WILL MAKE A MAN FEEL BAD.

4. I GOT A TWO·TIMIN' WOMAN, AND SHE'S THE WORST AROUN'.
   I'M GONNA GRAB ME A TRAIN, GONNA GET OUT OF THIS TOWN.

LONG, TALL DADDY

(SLOWLY)

1. I'VE GOT A SNOOT-FUL OF WHIS-KEY AN' A HEAD FULL OF GIN; THE DOC SAYS IT WILL KILL ME, BUT HE DON'T SAY WHEN. I'M A LONG, TALL DADDY, AND MY HOME'S OUT WEST. I'M LOOK-IN' FOR THE WO-MAN THAT'LL LOVE ME THE BEST. 2. I HAD A BEST.

2. I HAD A GAL IN THE COUNTRY AND A GAL IN THE TOWN,
I GUESS I'VE HAD A GAL IN EV'RY PLACE AROUN'
I'M A LONG, TALL DADDY, AN' MY HOME'S OUT WEST.
I'M LOOKIN' FOR THE WOMAN THAT'LL LOVE ME THE BEST.

3. I'VE SEEN THE GALS DOWN IN MEXICO AND IN TENNESSEE,
BUT I AIN'T FOUND THE ONE THAT REALLY SUITED ME.
I'M A LONG, TALL DADDY, AND MY HOME'S OUT WEST.
I'M LOOKIN' FOR THE WOMAN THAT'LL LOVE ME THE BEST.

4. I HAD A GAL BACK AT HOME WHO SAID THAT SHE LOVED ME SO,
SHE MAY HAVE TOLD THE TRUTH, OH, LORDY, I DON'T KNOW.
I'M A LONG, TALL DADDY, AND MY HOME'S OUT WEST.
I'M LOOKIN' FOR THE WOMAN THAT'LL LOVE ME THE BEST.

LONG TALL WOMAN

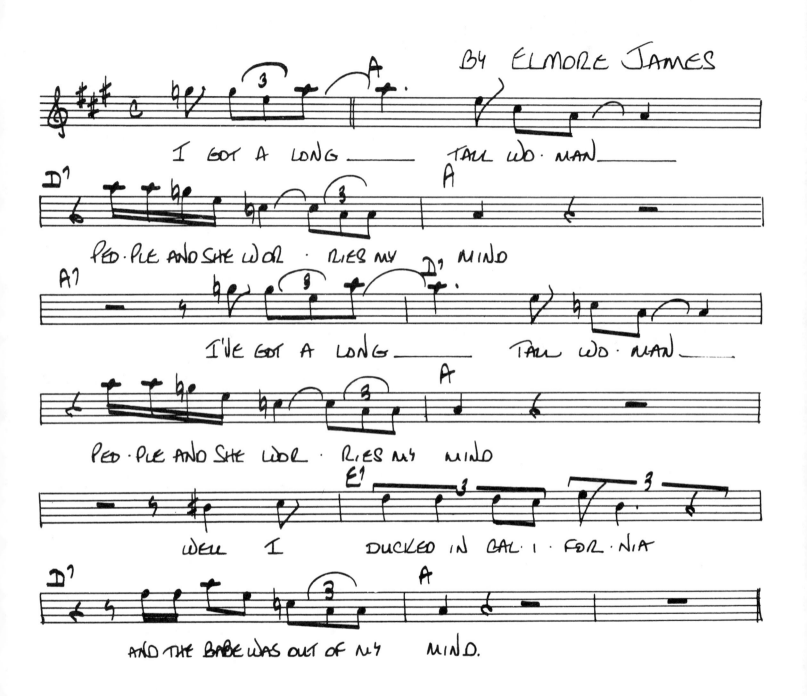

LONG WAY FROM HOME

BY LIGHTNIN' SAM HOPKINS

AN·Y TIME I TAKE A   TRIP DOWN SOUTH·A·WAYS

BABE, I MAY TAKE YOU WITH ME   TOO

AN·Y TIME I TAKE A   TRIP DOWN SOUTH·A·WAYS

BABE, I MAY TAKE YOU WITH ME   TOO

YEAH BUT TWO OR THREE PEO·PLE KEEP TELL·IN' ME

WHAT IN THE WORLD DO THEY WANT US TO DO.

2) LAST TIME I'M GONNA TELL YOU, LITTLE GIRL _ SOMEBODY'S
GOTTA GO

LAST TIME I'M GONNA TELL YOU, LITTLE GIRL _ SOMEBODY'S
GOTTA GO

YOU KNOW IT MAYBE YOU OR ME, BABY, EITHER ONE OF US
SURE DON'T KNOW

LOVE ME THIS MORNING

BY LIGHTNIN' SAM HOPKINS

LOVE ME THIS MOR-NIN'   OLD LIGHT-NIN'S

FIX-ING TO GO A-WAY   LOVE ME THIS MOR-NIN'

"OLE" LIGHT-NIN' HERE IS FIX-ING TO GO A-WAY

I MAY NOT BE GONE FOR-EV-ER

BUT I'M TRYIN' TO MAKE IT UP IN MY MIND TO STAY

2) TELL ME, BABY, LITTLE GIRL, HAVE YOU GOT ANYTHING ELSE TO SAY
TELL ME, LITTLE GIRL, HAVE YOU GOT ANYTHING ELSE TO SAY
"OLE" LIGHTNIN' HE GOING AWAY TO LEAVE YOU
THIS TIME, "OLE" LIGHTNIN' HE MAY STAY.

Lovin' Arms

By Lightnin' Sam Hopkins

Lucky Number Blues

(SLOWLY)

1. YOU HIT THE LUCK·Y NUM·BER, NOW YOU GOT PLEN·TY OF DOUGH, ___

___ YOU HIT THE LUCK·Y NUM·BER, NOW YOU GOT PLEN·TY OF DOUGH;

YOU'VE GOT A YOUNG·ER GAL NOW,

1.2.3.4, 5.

YOU DON'T WANT ME 'ROUND HERE NO MO? ___ 2. WHEN ___

2. WHEN I FIRST MET YOU, DADDY, YOU DIDN'T HAVE A DIME,
  I "GAVE" YOU "PLENTY" "MONEY," "YOU" "WERE" "MOOCHIN'" "ALL" "OF" "THE" TIME.

3. WHEN YOU WAS JUST A NOTHIN', I FED YOU GOOD EV'RY DAY,
  BUT NOW YOU'RE "IN" THE "BLUE" "CHIPS," "YOU" "SAY" "THAT" "I'M" "JUST" "IN" THE WAY.

4. WHEN YOU WERE COLD AND HUNGRY, I TRIED TO TREAT YOU KIND,
  " YOU " TOLD " ME " THAT " YOU " LOVED " ME, NOW YOU GONE AND CHANGED YOUR MIND.

5. I'M GONNA PACK MY SUITCASE, I'M GONNA SAY SO LONG,
  " I " TRIED " TO BE " A " GOOD " GAL, " BUT " MY " MAN HAS TREATED ME WRONG.

MAKE MY DREAMS COME TRUE

BY J. TAUB

I'm in love with the one _____ She's in love with my best
Won't you tell me baby _____ where you spent last
I got a fine lookin' woman _____ she lives clear 'cross
Well I love my baby _____ tell the world I

Friend _____ I'm in love with the one _____
Night _____ won't you tell me ba-by _____
Town _____ I got a fine lookin' woman _____
Do _____ well I love my baby _____

_____ She's in love with my best friend _____ Well
_____ where you spent last night _____ Well
_____ she lives clear 'cross town _____ And
_____ tell the world I do _____ Give me

Now we're real-ly through _____ All got-ta start all o-ver a-
You didn't come home _____ until the sun was shin-in'
When I'm with my baby _____ don't want no one else a-
A little love darlin' _____ and make my dreams come

gain. _____
bright. _____
round. _____
true. _____

MEAN AND EVIL

BY ELMORE JAMES
AND J. TAUB

My ba-by's so mean an' e-vil

I don't know what to do

My ba-by's so mean an' e-vil

I don't know what to do

Treat me low down an' dirty_ I

Can't get a-long with you

Well I lived in a small town_

WAS SO NICE AN' NEAT

WELL, I LIVED IN A SMALL TOWN, BABE

WAS SO NICE AN' NEAT

I BROUGHT YOU TO CHI·CA·GO

YOU DON'T DO NOTH·IN' BUT WALK THE STREET

WELL SHE USED TO COOK MY BREAK·FAST AND BRING IT TO MY BED SHE

USED TO WASH MY FACE AND EV·EN COMB MY HEAD___ SHE'S SO EVIL

I DON'T KNOW WHAT TO DO TREAT ME SO

LOW DOWN AN' DIR·TY I CAN'T GET A·LONG WITH YOU

MICHIGAN WATER BLUES

(MODERATE BLUES TEMPO)

1. MICH·I·GAN WA·TER TASTES LIKE SHER·RY WINE. SWEET SHER·RY

WINE, OH,— MIS·SIS·SIP·PI WA·TER,— TASTES LIKE I·O·DINE.

MICH·I·GAN WA·TER TASTES LIKE SHER·RY WINE._____

CRACK·IN' THE WHIP__ BUT THE MULE WON'T GO__ I JUST GOT·TA LEAVE HERE 'FORE THE

WIN·TER SNOW.__ MICH·I·GAN WA·TER TASTES LIKE SHER·RY WINE,

MICH·I·GAN WA·TER TASTES LIKE SHER·RY WINE._____

2.+3. MICHIGAN WATER TASTES LIKE SHERRY WINE. SWEET SHERRY WINE,
OH, MISSISSIPPI WATER TASTES LIKE IODINE
MICHIGAN WATER TASTES LIKE SHERRY WINE, *

*2. MISSING THAT GIRL THAT I CAN'T FORGET,
   I JUST GOTTA GET BACK, SHE'S MY ONLY BET,
*3. LIVIN' IT HIGH ON THE BIG OLD HOG
   JUST GOTTA LEAVE THIS LONDON FOG.

MICHIGAN WATER TASTES LIKE SHERRY WINE. (2x)

Mistreated Blues

By Lightnin' Sam Hopkins
& Jules Taub

Midnight Special

(MEDIUM ROCK TEMPO)

You get up in the morn·in'___ you hear the ding·dong ring.

Now you look__ up on a ta·ble you see the same damn__ thing.

You find no food up·on that ta·ble__ noth·ing__ up in the pan__ but if you say a thing a·bout it__

you'd be in trou·ble with the man___

CHORUS:

A· let the mid·night spe·cial__ shine her light on me__

___ oh, let the mid·night spe·cial___

shine her ev·er lov·in' light on me. ___ (well if you're ever in)

LIGHT ON ME. _____

2. WELL IF YOU'RE EVER IN HOUSTON, YOU'D BETTER WALK ON BY
OH, YOU'D BETTER NOT GAMBLE, BOY, I SAY YOU'D BETTER NOT FIGHT.
WELL NOW, THE SHERIFF, HE'LL GRAB YOU AND HIS BOYS WILL PULL YOU DOWN
AND THEN BEFORE YOU KNOW IT YOU'RE PENITENTIARY· BOUND. (·CHORUS·)

3. HERE COMES MISS LUCY HOW IN THE WORLD DO YOU KNOW?
I KNOW BY HER APRON AND BY THE DRESS SHE WORE.
AN UMBRELLA ON HER SHOULDER A PIECE OF PAPER IN HER HAND
SHE GONNA SEE THE SHERIFF TO TRY TO FREE HER MAN. (·CHORUS·)

MULE SKINNER BLUES

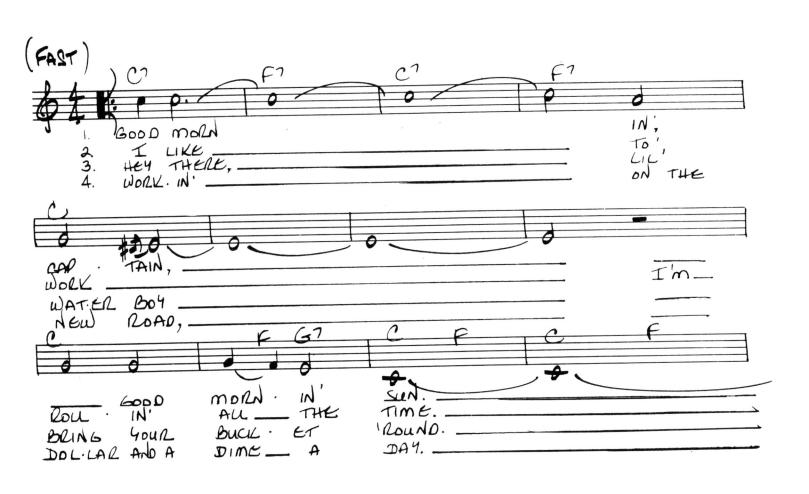

MORNING BLUES

By Lightnin' Sam Hopkins
& Stan Lewis

You know I went down to my ba·by's house fell down on my knees crying please_ please help poor me_ help old me_

2) She said Lightnin' I wished I was rich and you were poor
The meals that you've been getting, I will see that you never get them no more
She's talking to me and I'm down on bended knee
Somebody help me. Help me, please

3) You know I went to my house, wasn't nobody there but me
That was trouble, that was worry, Lord, Lord, like the whole world would see
Somebody, please, help me, I've been wondering about my fate
Her little smiling, baby, I can't see.

4) Well I'm about to make it up in my mind to let her go ahead on
Baby, you go have a good time, while I walk my floor and moan
You may not miss me now, but you're gonna miss me when I'm gone
Well I just can't do nothing but cry
I just got to walk my floor and moan

The Music's Hot

By James Moore
and Roy Hayes

(1.) I got one foot in the grave I

gave a great big shout Saint Peter, I can't

go tonight. We got a brand new rock'n sock 'em

record out! He said: "Son, where you goin'?"

Where the music's hot! Said: "Son, where you

goin'?" Where the music's hot!

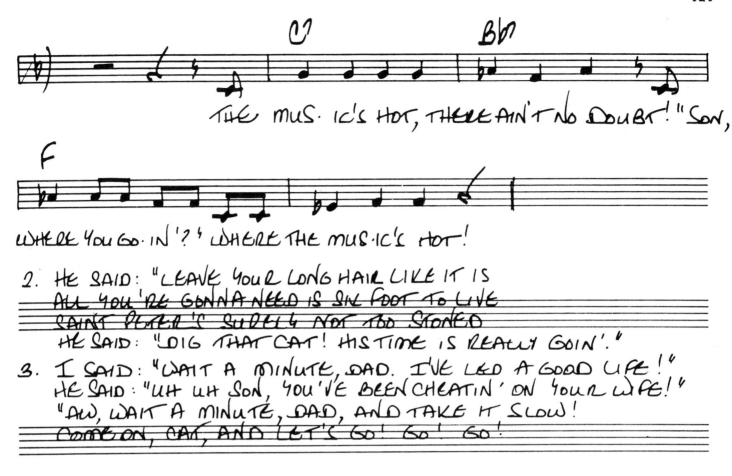

THE MUS·IC'S HOT, THERE AIN'T NO DOUBT! "SON,

WHERE YOU GO·IN'?" WHERE THE MUS·IC'S HOT!

2. HE SAID: "LEAVE YOUR LONG HAIR LIKE IT IS
~~ALL YOU'RE GONNA NEED IS SIX FOOT TO LIVE~~
~~SAINT PETER'S SURELY NOT TOO STONED~~
HE SAID: "DIG THAT CAT! HIS TIME IS REALLY GOIN'."

3. I SAID: "WAIT A MINUTE, DAD. I'VE LED A GOOD LIFE!"
HE SAID: "UH UH SON, YOU'VE BEEN CHEATIN' ON YOUR WIFE!"
"AW, WAIT A MINUTE, DAD, AND TAKE IT SLOW!
~~COME ON, CAT, AND LET'S GO! GO! GO!~~

MY BABY SHE'S GOT IT

BY JAMES MOORE

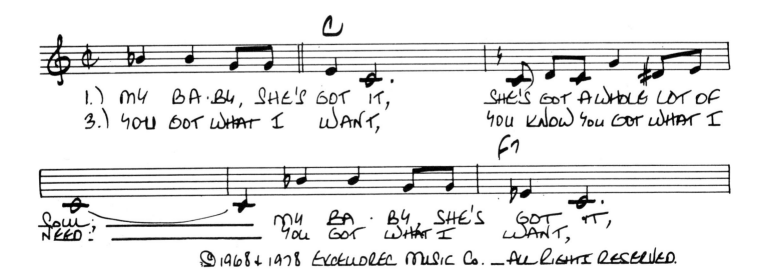

1.) MY BA·BY, SHE'S GOT IT;   SHE'S GOT A WHOLE LOT OF
3.) YOU GOT WHAT I WANT,   YOU KNOW YOU GOT WHAT I

YOU NEED? ____ MY BA·BY, SHE'S GOT IT,
YOU GOT WHAT I WANT,

My Suggestion

By Lightnin' Sam Hopkins

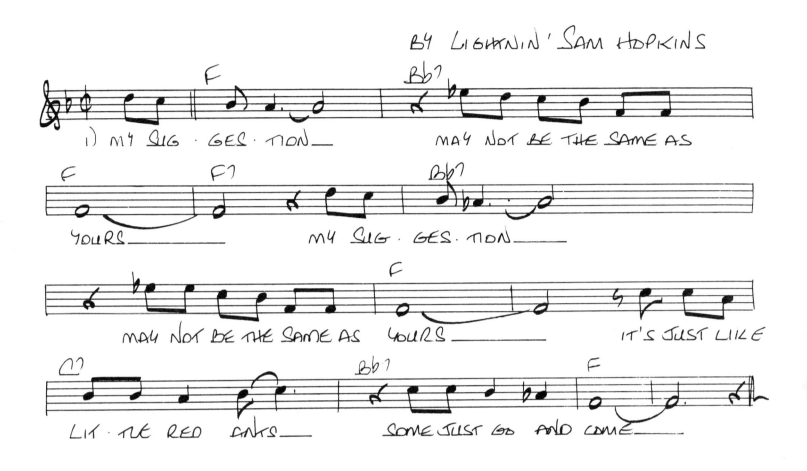

1) My sug-ges-tion___ may not be the same as yours___ my sug-ges-tion___ may not be the same as yours___ it's just like lit-tle red ants___ some just go and come___

2) Tell me, baby, do you know where you're at right now
Tell me, baby, do you know where you're at right now
She said, "I'm just thinkin' out in this lonesome world somewhere."

3) But if I lose you, darlin', I gotta go and look for me another
friend
Oh, if I lose you, darlin', I gotta go and look for me another
friend
Then I might have to tell the good Lord___ Lord this is the end

My Babe

BY WILLIE DIXON

QUARTER PAST NINE

BY ELMORE JAMES

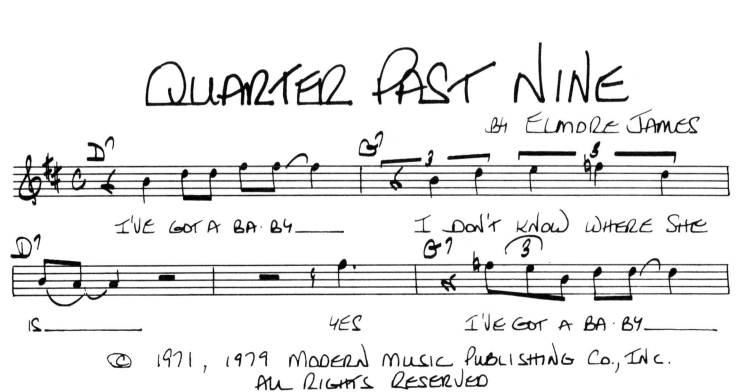

126

THE CLOCK HERE THIS MORNING SAY A QUARTER PAST NINE
I WAS SITTING AND ROCKING IN THE MORNING BABY
UNTIL A QUARTER PAST NINE
WELL WHEN I FIND MY OTHER BABY
YOU KNOW YOU DONE LOST YOUR TIME

New Stranger's Blues

I'm a stran-ger here, just blowed in your town;

I'm a stran-ger here, just blowed in your town;

Just be-cause I'm a stranger ev'ry-bod-y wants to dog ___ me

'round. Lord, I Blues. _____

Lord, I wonder do my good gal know I'm here; (2x)
Well, if she do, she sure don't seem to care.

I wonder how can some people dog a poor stranger so, (2x)
They should remember, they goin' to reap just what they sow.

I would stay up north but there's nothing here I can do, (2x)
But hang around this corner and sing the new stranger's blues.

Mama, I am going back south if I wear ninety-nine pairs of shoes (2x)

Then I know I'll be welcome and I won't have the new stranger's blues.

No Love In My Heart

By Joe Josea

YOU'RE JUST LIKE THE DEV-IL / NO LOVE IN MY HEART FOR
I'M GO-IN' BACK HOME / TELL YOU WHAT I'M GON-NA
I WAS A FOOL / TO BELIEVE WHAT YOU

YOU ___ / YOU'RE JUST LIKE THE DEV-IL
DO ___ / I'M GO-IN' BACK HOME
SAID ___ / I WAS A FOOL

NO LOVE IN MY HEART FOR / YOU ___ / I'M GO-IN' BACK
TELL YOU WHAT I'M GON-NA / DO ___ / I'M GONNA GET ME ANOTHER
TO BELIEVE WHAT YOU / SAID ___ / NOW I'M TIRED OF YOU TREATIN'

HOME ___ / NOTH-IN' I CAN DO WITH
WOMAN ___ / BECAUSE I CAN'T USE
ME ___ / LIKE SOME BUM LOOKIN'

YOU. ___
YOU. ___
BAD. ___

One Kind Favor

By Lightnin' Sam Hopkins
& Jules Taub

Peace of Mind

By B. B. King and J. Josea

Please Find My Baby

By Elmore James and Joe Josea

Rabbit-Foot Blues

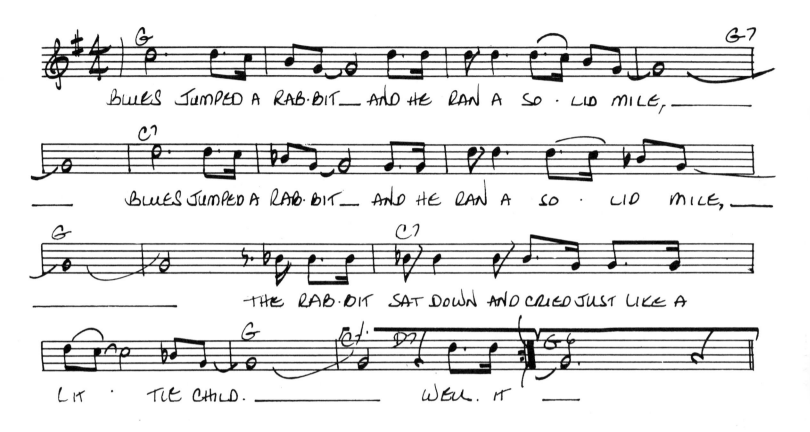

BLUES JUMPED A RAB-BIT AND HE RAN A SO-LID MILE,

BLUES JUMPED A RAB-BIT AND HE RAN A SO-LID MILE,

THE RAB-BIT SAT DOWN AND CRIED JUST LIKE A

LIT-TLE CHILD. WELL, IT

WELL, IT SEEMS LIKE YOU'RE HUNGRY, WHY DON'T YOU COME AND LUNCH WITH ME?

I'M GONNA STOP THESE MARRIED-LOOKIN' WIMMEN FROM WORRYIN' ME.

I HAVE UNEEDA BISCUITS AND A HALF PINT OF GIN,

THE GIN IS MIGHTY FINE, THEM BISCUITS IS A LITTLE TOO THIN.

BABY, TELL ME SOMETHING ABOUT MEATLESS AND WHEATLESS DAYS,

THIS NOT BEING MY HOME, I DON'T THINK I SHOULD STAY.

WELL, I CRIED FOR FLOUR; MEAT, I DECLARE, WAS GONE.

PEOPLE FEED ME CORN BREAD, I JUST CAN'T STICK AROUND HOME.

GOT A KNAPSACK, BABY, AND I'M GONNA GET A SUBMARINE,

GONNA GET THAT KAISER BY 1917.

Rainin' In My Heart

By James Moore
and Jerry West

Ride in Your New Automobile

By Lightnin' Sam Hopkins

1) I SAW YOU RIDING A-ROUND
IN YOUR BRAND NEW AUTO-MO-BILE
I SAW YOU RIDING A-ROUND
YOU RIDING A-ROUND IN YOUR BRAND NEW AU-TO-MO-BILE
YEAH— SHE WAS SIT-TING THERE HAP-PY WITH HER HAND-SOME
DRI—VER AT THE WHEEL IN YOUR BRAND
NEW AU-TO-MO-BILE

YES IF I LUCK UP ON MY SHOTGUN AGAIN
HE WON'T BE YOUR DRIVER NO MORE ALL RIGHT BOYS ALL RIGHT BOYS
2) NOW IF YOU LOVE ME BABY YOU'LL LET ME DRIVE YOUR LITTLE AUTOMOBILE
IF YOU LOVE ME IF YOU LOVE ME YOU'LL LET ME DRIVE YOUR LITTLE AUTOMOBILE
YES I GOT A CINCH ON MY DRIVING
I WON'T HAVE NO WRECK AT YOUR WHEEL IN YOUR BRAND NEW AUTOMOBILE.

Rock Me Baby

By B. B. King and J. Josea

(Moderately, with Soul)

Rock me, ba-by, Rock me all night long _____ Rock me, ba-by, Rock me all night long _____ I want you to rock me, ba-by, like my back ain't got no bones _____ Roll me, ba-by,

LIKE YOU ROLL A WAG·ON   WHEEL _____

ROLL ME, BA·BY,   LIKE YOU ROLL A   WAG·ON

WHEEL _____   I WANT YOU TO ROLL ME, BA·BY _____

YOU DON'T KNOW HOW IT MAKES ME   FEEL. _____

ROCK ME BABY, ROCK ME BABY SO
ROCK ME BABY, ROCK ME BABY SO
I WANT YOU TO ROCK ME, BABY,
TILL I DON'T WANT NO MORE.

ROCK ME MAMA

By Lightnin' Sam Hopkins

JUST ROCK ME, MA-MA,   ROCK ME, BA-BY,

ROCK ME ALL NIGHT LONG   ROCK ME, BA-BY,

ROCK ME ALL NIGHT LONG

I WANT YOU TO BE IN YOUR   LIKE YOUR BACK AIN'T GOT NO BONE!

2) SEE ME COMIN', GO GET YOUR ROCKING CHAIR
SEE ME COMIN', BABY, GO GET YOUR ROCKIN' CHAIR
YOU KNOW I AIN'T NO STRANGER
"OLE" LIGHTNIN' ONCE LIVED OVER HERE.

ROCK MY BABY RIGHT

BY ELMORE JAMES
& JOE JOSEA

MY BA·BY'S GOT WAYS I JUST CAN'T UN·DER·STAND
I SAID BABY BABY PLEASE COME BACK TO ME
MY BABY'S GOT SOMETHING THAT SHINES LIKE THE RISIN' SUN

MY BA·BY'S GOT WAYS I JUST CAN'T UN·DER·
I SAID BABY BABY PLEASE COME BACK TO
MY BABY'S GOT SOMETHING THAT SHINES LIKE THE RISIN'

STAND
ME
SUN

LEAVES ME IN THE MORN·IN'
I'LL MAKE YOU AS HAPPY
YOU'RE THE SWEETEST THING
WAKE UP IN THE MORN·IN'

GOES WITH AN·OTH·ER MAN
AS ANY LIT·TLE GIRL CAN BE
I HAVE EVER SEEN
MY LOVE HAS JUST BEGUN

I GOT·TA ROCK MY BA·BY RIGHT ROCK MY BA·BY TIGHT

WAKE UP IN THE MORN·IN' LOVE MY BA·BY ALL NIGHT GOT·TA
HOLD MY BA·BY IN MY ARMS AND LOVE HER ALL THIS NIGHT

ROCK MY BA·BY ROCK MY BA·BY

ROCK MY BA·BY ROCK MY BA·BY ALL NIGHT.

Santa Fe Blues

BY JULES TAUB

Sho Nuf I Do

BY ELMORE JAMES
& JOE JOSEA

WELL I CAME HOME ONE MORNIN' FOUND MY BA-BY
FIRST TIME I SAW HER ON A FRI-DAY
I SAW HER ONE MORN-IN' SHE WAS GOIN' ROUND THE
I RAISE MY HANDS ONCE A-

GONE _____ WELL YOU KNOW I AL-WAYS _____ LIVED ALL A-
NIGHT _____ I TOLD HER BA-BY _____ I TOLD HER
STREET _____ SHE WAS SHAKIN' HANDS _____ WITH EVERY MAN
-GAIN _____ BABY IF YOU PLEASE BABY _____ PLEASE UNDER-

LONE
EVERYTHING WAS ALRIGHT
SHE MEET } OH, I LOVE HER _____ YES I
-STAND

LOVE HER _____ SHO NUFF I DO _____

See See Rider

Shake Your Hips

By James Moore

1.) I WAN·NA TELL YOU 'BOUT A DANCE   THAT'S GOIN' A-
2.) _ NOW_ PLEASE _DON'T_ GO,   DON'T BE   A-
3.) _ I _ MET A LIT·TLE GIRL   IN A COUN·TRY

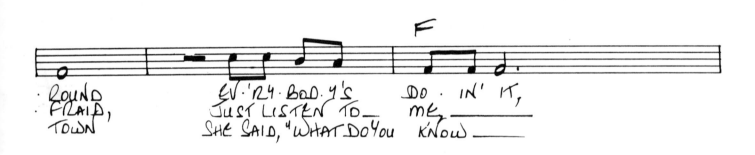

·ROUND   EV·'RY·BOD·Y'S   DO·IN' IT,
FRAID,   JUST LISTEN TO_   ME_____
TOWN   SHE SAID, "WHAT DO YOU   KNOW _____

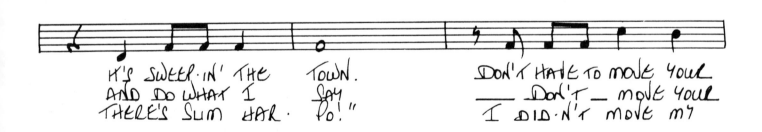

IT'S SWEEP·IN' THE   TOWN.   DON'T HAVE TO MOVE YOUR
AND DO WHAT I   SAY,   _ DON'T_ MOVE YOUR
THERE'S SLIM HAR·PO!"   I DID·N'T MOVE MY

145

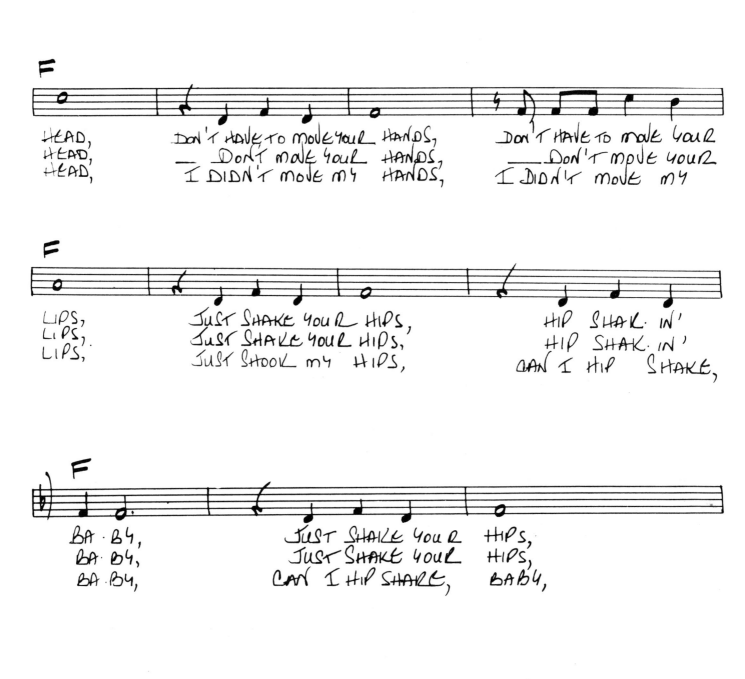

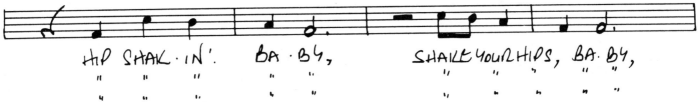

Shake Yours

BY B. B. KING AND
J. TAUB

(MODERATELY)

HEL·LO BA·BY, I'M SO GLAD TO BE BACK.

GOT NEWS FOR YOU, BA·BY, THAT'S A NAT·'RAL FACT

SINCE I AM BACK, LET'S

GET IN·TO OUR ACT.

LOVE YOU, BA·BY, MORE THAN WORDS CAN SAY

147

Sinful Woman

By Elmore James
& Sam Ling

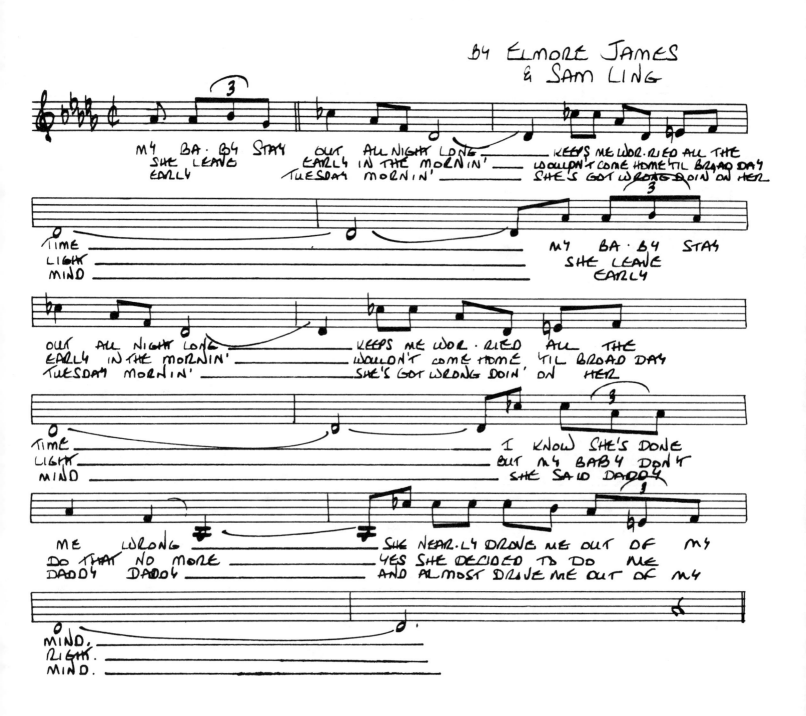

So Mean To Me

BY ELMORE JAMES AND SAM LING

OH BA·BY____ YOU'RE SO MEAN TO ME____

OH BA·BY____

YOU'RE SO MEAN TO ME____ GOT·TA

LEAVE YOU BA·BY__ YOU KNOW I GOT TO LET YOU

BE.

Some Day Baby

BY LIGHTNIN' SAM HOPKINS

OH LORD-Y / LORD _____ OH LORD-Y / LORD _____ HURTS YOU GO
SHE'S ON MY / MIND _____ SHE'S ON MY MIND _____ EV'RY PLACE I
SO MAN-Y / NIGHTS _____ SINCE YOU BEEN GONE _____ I BEEN
AND MY / STORY _____ HERE'S ALL I GOT TO SAY _____ GOOD BYE

BAD
GO _____ FOR US TO PART _____ HOW MUCH I LOVE HERE NOBODY KNOWS _____
WONDERIN' _____ HOW MY LIFE GOES ON _____ } BUT SOME-DAY
BABY _____ DON'T CARE WHAT YOU DO _____

BA-BY _____ YOU AIN'T GON-NA WORRY MY LIFE ANY-

MORE _____

Sportin' Life Blues

I GOT A LET·TER FROM MY HOME, MOST OF MY FRIENDS ARE DEAD AND GONE; THAT OLD NIGHT LIFE. THAT SPORT·IN' LIFE IS KILL· IN' ME.

MY MOTH·ER

MY MOTHER USED TO SAY TO ME, "SO YOUNG AND FOOLISH, THAT I CAN'T SEE."
AIN'T GOT NO MOTHER, MY SISTER AND BROTHER WON'T TALK TO ME.

I'VE BEEN A LIAR AND A CHEATER TOO, SPENT ALL MY MONEY AND BOOZE ON YOU;
THAT OLD NIGHT LIFE, THAT SPORTIN' LIFE IS KILLIN' ME.

MY MOTHER USED TO SAY TO ME, "SO YOUNG AND FOOLISH, THAT I CAN'T SEE.
HO, JERRY, HEY THERE, JERRY, WHY DON'T YOU CHANGE YOUR WAYS?"

I'VE BEEN A GAMBLER AND A CHEATER TOO, BUT NOW IT'S COME MY TURN TO LOSE,
THIS OLD SPORTIN' LIFE HAS GOT THE BEST HAND, WHAT CAN I DO?

THERE AIN'T BUT ONE THING THAT I'VE DONE WRONG, LIVED THIS SPORTIN' LIFE
MY FRIEND, TOO LONG;
I SAY IT'S NO GOOD, PLEASE BELIEVE ME, PLEASE LEAVE IT ALONE.

I'M GETTIN' TIRED OF RUNNIN' 'ROUND, THINK I WILL MARRY AND SETTLE DOWN,
THAT OLD NIGHT LIFE, THAT SPORTIN' LIFE IS KILLIN' ME.

St. James Infirmary

(MODERATE, BLUES STYLE)

STANDING AT THE CROSSROADS

BY ELMORE JAMES
& JOE JOSEA

WELL I'M STANDIN' AT THE CROSSROADS _____ WITH MY HEAD HUNG DOWN AND
I WORK HARD FOR MY BABY _____ AND SHE TREATS ME LIKE A
WELL I'M STANDIN' AT THE CROSSROADS _____ AND MY BABY'S NOT A
I'M STANDIN' HERE WAITIN' BABY _____ WITH MY HEART RIGHT IN MY

CRYIN' _____ WELL I'M
SLAVE _____ I WORK
ROUND _____ WELL I'M
HAND _____ I'M STANDIN'

STANDIN' AT THE CROSSROADS _____ WITH MY HEAD HUNG DOWN AND
HARD FOR MY BABY _____ AND SHE TREATS ME LIKE A
STANDIN' AT THE CROSSROADS _____ AND MY BABY'S NOT A
HERE WAITIN' BABY _____ WITH MY HEART RIGHT IN MY

CRYIN' _____ WELL I WAS
SLAVE _____ WELL SHE WAS
ROUND _____ I BEGAN TO
HAND _____ I'M THINKIN'

THINKIN' ABOUT MY BABY _____ AND I KNOW SHE CAN'T BE
BE TIRED OF LIVIN' _____ I'LL PUT HER SIX FEET IN THE
WONDER _____ IF THIS IS ELMORE'S SECOND
ABOUT MY BABY _____ AND SHE'S OUT WITH ANOTHER

FOUND. _____
GRAVE. _____
DOWN. _____
MAN. _____

STEP IT UP AND GO

1. USED TO HAVE A GAL SHE WAS LIT·TLE AND LOW,— SHE USED TO LOVE ME BUT SHE DON'T NO MORE, SHE HAD TO

(CHORUS:)
STEP IT UP AND GO ____ YEAH,— GO! ____

(1. ONLY)
SHE COULDN'T STAY THERE, I DE·
(I)

CLARE SHE HAD TO STEP IT UP AND GO!

2. OUT WITH A WOMAN, HAVIN' SOME FUN, IN COME A MAN WITH A GREAT, BIG GUN
   I HAD TO STEP IT UP AND GO, (CHORUS:)

3. JUMPED IN THE RIVER, TRIED TO GET ACROSS, JUMPED ON AN ALLIGATOR,
   THOUGHT IT WAS A HORSE
   I HAD TO STEP IT UP AND GO, (CHORUS:)

4. TWO OLD MAIDS, SITTIN' IN THE SAND, EACH ONE WISHIN' THAT THE
   OTHER WAS A MAN
   STEP IT UP AND GO, (CHORUS:)

5. I'M SO GLAD THE WORLD'S ROUND LIKE A BALL, THERE'S ENOUGH
   PRETTY WOMAN HERE FOR US ALL
   WE GOT TO STEP IT UP AND GO, (CHORUS:)

Strange Kinda Feeling

By Elmore James
& Joe Josea

Sugar Babe Blues

TAKE YOUR ARM FROM 'ROUND MY NECK — SUG-AR BABE, —

TAKE YOUR ARM FROM 'ROUND MY NECK — SUG-AR BABE, —

TAKE YOUR ARM FROM 'ROUND MY NECK, — YOU'RE A

DIR-TY LIT-TLE IN-SECT. — I'M GON-NA SEND YOU BACK TO

GEOR-GIA SUGAR BABE. — I PULLED —

I PULLED YOU BEFORE YOU GOT RIGHT — SUGAR BABE (2X)
I PULLED YOU BEFORE YOU GOT RIGHT, NOW I KNOW YOU AIN'T MY TYPE;
I'M GONNA SEND YOU BACK TO GEORGIA — SUGAR BABE.

I BOUGHT YOU CLOTHES IN THE LATEST STYLE — SUGAR BABE, (2X)
I BOUGHT YOU CLOTHES IN THE LATEST STYLE,
HELL YOU ARE RUNNING WILD.
I'M GONNA SEND YOU BACK TO GEORGIA — SUGAR BABE.

I GOT ENOUGH OF YOUR BABY TALK — SUGAR BABE, (2X)
I GOT ENOUGH OF YOUR BABY TALK; HERE'S YOUR FARE, YOU DON'T
                                    HAVE TO WALK
I'M GONNA SEND YOU BACK TO GEORGIA — SUGAR BABE.

Sweet Little Angel

By B.B. King and
J. Taub

Sweet Sixteen

By B. B. King and J. Josea

(Moderately)

1. WHEN I FIRST MET YOU, BA-BY, BA-BY, YOU WERE JUST ____ SWEET SIX-
2. BUT YOU WOULDN'T DO NOTHING, BA-BY, YOU WOULDN'T DO ANY-THING I ASK YOU
3. YOU KNOW I LOVE YOU, BA-BY, I LOVED YOU BE-FORE I COULD CALL YOUR
4. WELL MY BROTH-ER'S IN VIET-NAM, SIS-TER'S DOWN IN ____ NEW OR-
5. YOU KNOW I LOVE YOU AND I'LL DO AN-Y-THING YOU ____ TELL ME
6. YOU CAN TREAT ME MEAN, BA-BY BUT I'LL KEEP LOV-ING YOU ____ JUST THE

TEEN ____ WHEN I FIRST MET YOU, BA-BY,
TO ____ YES YOU WOULDN'T DO NOTHING, BA-BY,
NAME ____ YOU KNOW I LOVE YOU, BA-BY,
LEANS ____ WELL MY BROTH-ER'S IN VIET-NAM,
TO ____ YOU KNOW I LOVE YOU AND I'LL
SAME ____ YOU CAN TREAT ME MEAN, BA-BY,

BA-BY YOU WERE JUST ____ SWEET SIX-TEEN ____ YOU JUST LEFT YOUR
YOU WOULDN'T DO ANY-THING I ASK YOU TO ____ YOU KNOW YOU
I LOVED YOU BE-FORE I COULD CALL YOUR NAME ____ WELL, IT SEEMS LIKE
SIS-TER'S DOWN IN ____ NEW OR-LEANS ____ WELL, YOU KNOW, I'M
DO AN-Y-THING YOU ____ TELL ME TO ____ WELL, THERE AIN'T
BUT I'LL KEEP LOV-ING YOU ____ JUST THE SAME ____ BUT ONE OF THESE DAYS

HOME THEN, WO-MAN, OH ____ THE SWEETEST THING I'D EV-ER SEEN. ____
RUN AWAY FROM HOME, BABY, AND NOW YOU WANT TO RUN A-WAY FROM "OLD B" TOO. ____
EVERY-THING I DO BABY, EV-ERY-THING I DO IS IN VAIN.
HAVING SO MUCH TROUBLE, SOMETIMES I WONDER WHAT IN THE WORLD IS GOING TO HAPPEN TO ME.
NOTHING IN THE WORLD, WOMAN, THAT ____ I WOULDN'T DO FOR YOU, ____
YOU'RE GOING TO GIVE A LOT OF MONEY, JUST TO HEAR SOMEONE CALL MY NAME. ____

159

T. B. Blues

LOOK-IN' AT ME __ FROM MY HEAD TO MY FEET; __ OUT LORD, NOW __

_____ T. B.'S IS KILLIN' ME. _____

_____ YOU KNOW I'M LIKE A PRIS'NER, AL-WAYS WISH-IN' HE'S FREE __

T. B.'S IS __

T. B.S IS ALL RIGHT TO HAVE, BUT YOUR FRIENDS TREAT YOU SO LOW.
DOWN (2X)
DON'T YOU ASK THEM FOR A FAVOR, THEY'LL STOP COMING AROUND.

UMMM·MMM, T.B.S IS KILLIN' ME. (2X)
I WISH I WAS DEAD AND BURIED IN THE DEEP BLUE SEA.

T. B.S IS ALL RIGHT TO HAVE, BUT YOUR FRIENDS TREAT YOU SO
LOW. DOWN (2X)
DON'T YOU ASK THEM FOR A FAVOR, THEY'LL EVEN STOP COMING AROUND.

UMMM·MMM, T.B.S IS KILLIN' ME.
HOLLERIN' LORD __ T.B.S IS KILLIN' ME.
GOT THE TUBERCULOSIS, CONSUMPTION IS KILLIN' ME.

TAKE THIS HAMMER

(SLOWLY, WITH A HEAVY BEAT)

TAKE THIS HAM·MER, ___ CAR·RY IT TO THE
CAP·TAIN, ___ TAKE THIS HAM·MER, ___ CAR·RY IT TO THE
CAP·TAIN. ___ TAKE THIS HAM·MER, ___ CAR·RY IT TO THE
CAP·TAIN, ___ TELL HIM I'M GONE, ___ TELL HIM I'M GONE

IF HE ASKS YOU, WAS I LAUGHIN', (3x)
TELL HIM I WAS CRYIN', TELL HIM I WAS CRYIN'.

IF HE ASKS YOU, WAS I RUNNIN', (3x)
TELL HIM I WAS FLYIN', TELL HIM I WAS FLYIN'.

I DON'T WANT NO CORNBREAD AND MOLASSES, (3x)
THEY HURT MY PRIDE, THEY HURT MY PRIDE.

I DON'T WANT NO COLD IRON SHACKLES, (3x)
AROUND MY LEG, AROUND MY LEG.
    (REPEAT VERSE ONE)

Talkin' Some Sense

By Lightnin' Sam Hopkins

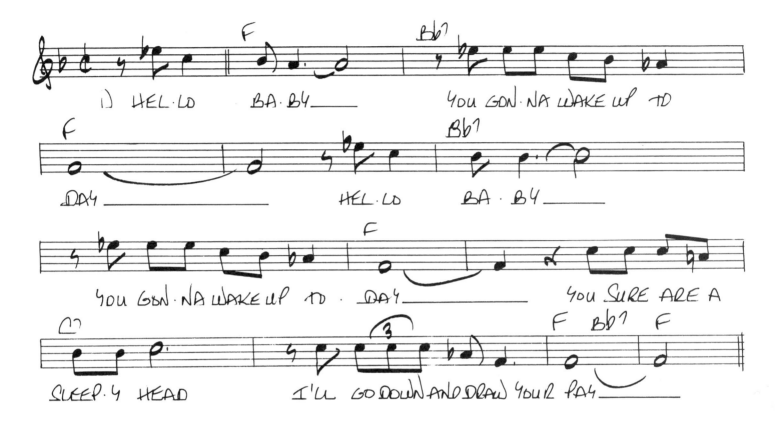

1) Hel-lo ba-by___ you gon-na wake up to day___ Hel-lo ba-by___ you gon-na wake up to-day___ you sure are a sleep-y head I'll go down and draw your pay___

2) I'm gonna take you back to your mama, little girl
   Maybe she can talk some sense in your head
   That's why I'm gonna carry you back to your dear ole
   mother___ she claims she can talk some sense
   into your head.

TE-NI-NEE-NI-NU

By JAMES MOORE

1.) I WANT YOU   TO BE MY TE-NI-NEE-NI NU,
2.) COME ON, BABY   AND SHAKE IT, YOU'VE GOT THE FLOOR,

I WANT YOU   TO BE MY TE-NI-NEE-NI-NU.
EV'RY-BODY'S   WATCHIN' YOU, YOU'RE LOOKIN' GOOD.

TELL ME THE TRUTH,   AIN'T YOU MY TE-NI-NEE-NI-NU?
NOW WHEN YOU'RE THRU   COME BE MY TE-NI-NEE-NI-NU.

NOW, WILL YOU LOVE,   WILL YOU HUG ME,   WILL YOU

SQUEEZE ME?   COME ON, DON'T TEASE ME,   TELL ME THE TRUTH,

AIN'T YOU MY TE-NI-NEE-NI-NU?

That Evil Child

By B. B. King and
J. Josea

(Slow, with Soul)

WHEN-EV-ER I TRY TO HOLD MY BA-BY, SHE JUST STAND THERE FOR A-WHILE

NO MAT-TER HOW I TRY TO PLEASE THAT WO-MAN, SHE WON'T EV-EN CRACK A SMILE__ LORD,

MAY-BE YOU IN HEAV-EN CAN HELP ME, 'CAUSE THIS IS ONE__ E-VIL

CHILD__ OH__ I SAID MAY-BE, MAY-BE SOME-BOD-Y HELP ME__

BE-CAUSE THIS IS__ ONE E-VIL CHILD.

THINGS ABOUT TO COME MY WAY

(SLOW BLUES)

2. THE POT WAS BOILIN' I DIDN'T CARE, THERE WASN'T NOTHING,
NO, NOTHING COOKING IN THERE.
NOW, AFTER ALL MY HARD TRAVELIN', THINGS ABOUT TO COME MY WAY.

3. OLD MULE GOT SICKLY, SHE WOULDN'T GO
I HAD TO WORK I DID THE PLOWIN' ALONE.
NOW, AFTER ALL MY HARD TRAVELIN', THINGS ABOUT TO COME MY WAY.

4. THE SUN IS SHININ' SOMEWHERE, I KNOW
SOMEDAY I'LL FIND IT, AND IT WILL MELT ALL THIS SNOW.
NOW AFTER ALL MY HARD TRAVELIN', THINGS ABOUT TO COME MY WAY.

Time To Say Goodbye

By B. B. King and S. Ling

(MODERATELY)

THERE WAS A TIME___ WHEN I LOVED YOU___ THAT WAS A

TIME, BABE___ YOU MADE ME BLUE, THERE'S A TIME___ EV'RYTHING MUST END,

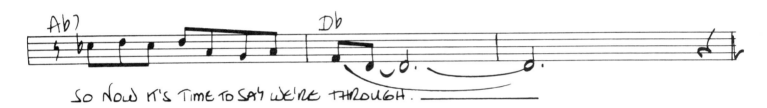

SO NOW IT'S TIME TO SAY WE'RE THROUGH. ___

2. REMEMBER THE TIME, THE TIME YOU MADE ME CRY
BUT NOW, BABY, YOU'RE BREAK MY HEART
THEY SAY THERE'S A TIME FOR EVERYTHING, BABY,
SO IT'S TIME THAT WE MUST PART.

3. REMEMBER THE TIME BABY, YOU MADE ME CRY
AND THE TIME, BABY, WHEN YOU BROKE MY HEART
BUT THERE'S A TIME FOR EVERYTHING, BABY,
SO NOW IT'S TIME WE MUST PART.

4. THEY SAY THAT TIME BRINGS ABOUT A CHANGE
AND I KNOW, BABY, I KNOW NOW IT IS NO LIE
THERE'S TIMES I'VE GOT TO FORGET YOU, BABY,
SO IT'S TIME TO SAY GOODBYE.

THREE O'Clock Blues

BY B. B. KING AND
J. TAUB

NOW HERE IT IS___THREE O'CLOCK IN THE MORN·ING

AND I CAN'T EV·EN CLOSE MY _____ EYES___

OH YES, IT'S THREE O'CLOCK IN THE MORN·ING, BA·BY___

I CAN'T EV·EN CLOSE MY EYES___

YOU KNOW I CAN'T FIND MY WO·MAN___

The Thrill Is Gone

BY ROY HAWKINS AND
RICK DARNEL

TIP ON IN

By James Moore
and R. Holmes

(SPOKEN:) OH, LAY IT ON ME, BABY, DON'T STOP NOW. LET YOUR HAIR DOWN, BABY, — WE AIN'T GOIN' TO HEAVEN NOHOW. I'M READY TO BURN, BABY, RIGHT HERE AND NOW. OH, I DIG THOSE CRAZY CLOTHES. LET ME FEEL THOSE FISH NET HOSE. GOT LOW AT THE TOP AND HIGH AT THE BOTTOM. IN FACT I DON'T SEE HOW WE EVER DID WITHOUT 'EM.

NOW, THERE'S A PLACE DOWN THE STREET THEY CALL THE "TIP ON IN". LET'S WALK ON DOWN THERE, BABY, THAT'S WHERE THE FUN BEGINS. BUT LET ME CHECK YOU JUST ONE MORE TIME. YOU KNOW YOU SEND ME, BABY, LET'S GO ON IN HERE. NOW SOCK IT TO ME. YOU KNOW IT'S GETTIN' GOOD TO ME NOW.

TROUBLES, TROUBLES, TROUBLES

BY B. B. KING AND
S. LING

(MODERATELY)

Trouble No More

WANDERIN'

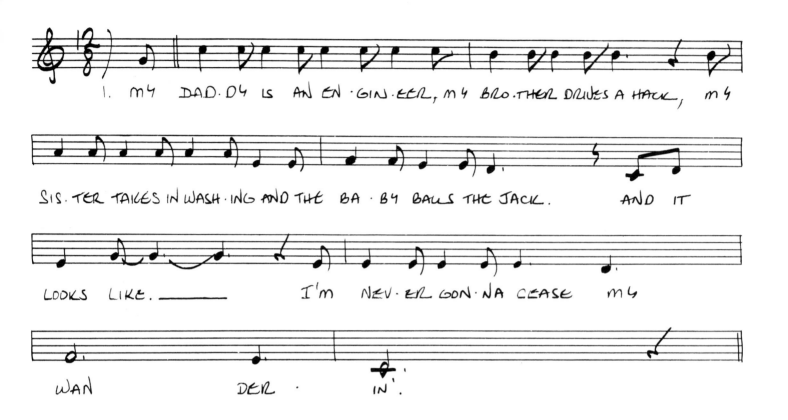

1. MY DAD·DY IS AN EN·GIN·EER, MY BRO·THER DRIVES A HACK, MY
SIS·TER TAKES IN WASH·ING AND THE BA·BY BALLS THE JACK. AND IT
LOOKS LIKE. _____ I'M NEV·ER GON·NA CEASE MY
WAN DER· IN'.

2. I'VE WORKED IN THE CITY, I'VE WORKED ON A FARM,
   AND ALL I GOT TO SHOW FOR IT'S THIS MUSCLE IN MY ARM.
   AND IT LOOKS LIKE I'M NEVER GONNA CEASE MY WANDERIN'.

3. THERE'S ROCKS IN THE MOUNTAINS, THERE'S ROCKS IN THE SEA,
   IT TOOK A RED·HEADED WOMAN TO MAKE A FOOL OUT OF ME.
   AND IT LOOKS LIKE I'M NEVER GONNA CEASE MY WANDERIN'.

4. I BEEN A WANDERIN' EARLY AND LATE,
   FROM NEW YORK CITY TO THE GOLDEN GATE.
   AND IT LOOKS LIKE I'M NEVER GONNA CEASE MY WANDERIN'.

WET WEATHER BLUES

(SLOWLY)

1. WELL, IT RAINED ALL THE MORNIN', AND THEN IT RAINED ALL NIGHT, ___
YES, IT RAINED ALL THE MORNIN', AND THEN IT RAINED ALL NIGHT; ___
WA-TER ALL 'ROUND THE CAB-IN. JUST AN AW-FUL SIGHT. ___
2. WHEN THE ___

2. WHEN THE WIND STARTED HOWLIN', I LIKE TO BLEW AWAY, (2x)
OH, IT SCARED ME SO AWFUL THAT I KNEELED DOWN TO PRAY.

3. LORDY, PLEASE LISTEN TO ME AND ROLL THEM CLOUDS AWAY, (2x)
'CAUSE THE SKY IS SO DARK, LOOKS LIKE JUDGMENT DAY.

4. THEM POOR FOLKS IN THE LOWLANDS, I KNOW THEY'RE GONNA DROWN, (2x)
'CAUSE THE WATER IS RISIN', COMIN' UP ALL AROUN'.

5. OH, THE LIGHTNIN' CAME FLASHIN', THE THUNDER MADE A ROAR,
YES, "   "   "   "   "   "   "   "   "   "
AND A TREE CAME A-CRASHIN', LIKE TO BUST MY DOOR.

6. IF THE SUN WAS A-SHININ', I WOULDN'T WORRY SO, 2x)
AND THE WET WEATHER BLUES WOULDN'T BE 'ROUND HERE NO MORE.

WHEN MY HEART BEATS LIKE A HAMMER

By B. B. KING,
J. TAUB AND S. LING

WHERE CAN MY BABY BE

BY ELMORE JAMES

WELL, IT'S SOON ___ IN THE MORN·ING ___

AND THE DAWN IS COV·ERED WITH SNOW

OH, IT'S SOON IN THE MORN·ING

AND THE DAWN IS COV·ERED WITH SNOW

OH, THE WO·MAN I LOVE DONE LEFT ME ___ AND I

AND I CAN'T FEEL GOOD NO MORE

WHOLE LOT OF LOVE

BY J. JOSEA AND
M. DAVIS

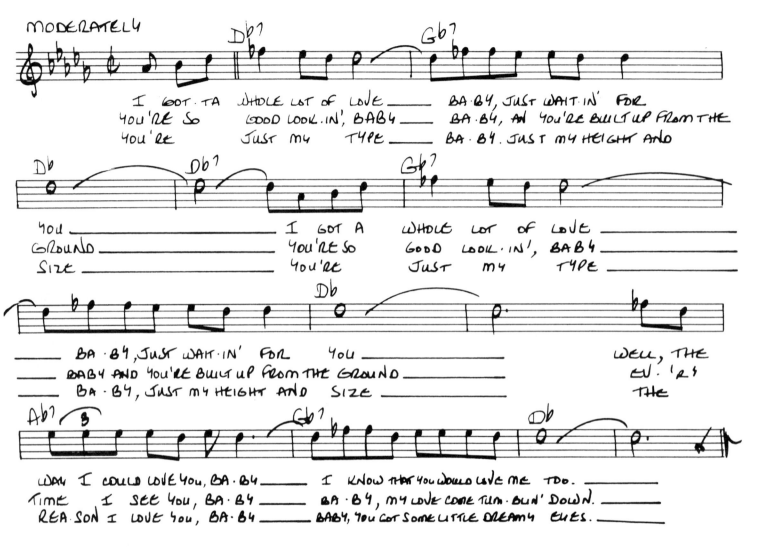

WILD ABOUT YOU BABY

BY ELMORE JAMES

WELL I'M WILD A·BOUT YOU BA·BY AND YOU JUST WON'T TREAT ME RIGHT

YES I'M WILD A·BOUT YOU BA·BY AND YOU JUST WON'T TREAT ME RIGHT YOU LEAVE HOME EAR·LY IN THE MORN·ING AND STAYS OUT ALL DAY LONG

WILLIE THE WEEPER

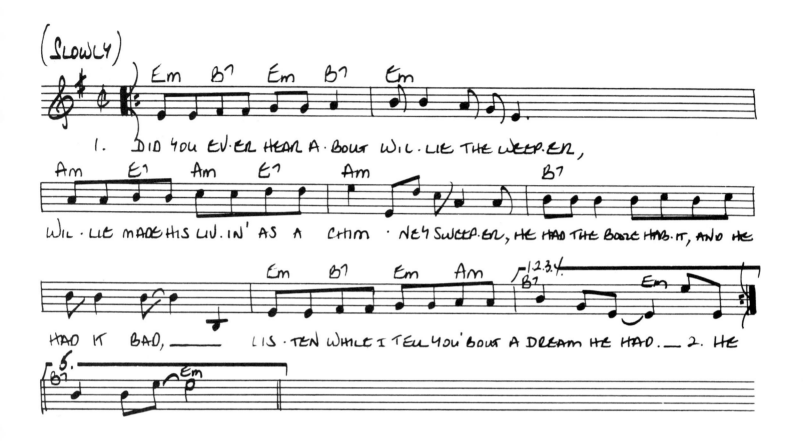

2. HE WENT DOWN TO THE CORNER ONE SATURDAY NIGHT,
   KNEW THAT ALL THE LIGHTS WOULD BE A·BURNIN' BRIGHT,
   I GUESS HE HAD SIX OR SEVEN DRINKS, OR MORE,
   WHEN HE WOKE UP HE WAS ON A FOREIGN SHORE.

3. THE QUEEN OF TIMBUCTOO WAS THE FIRST ONE HE MET,
   CALLED HIM TOOTSIE·WOOTSIE AND HER HONEY PET,
   SHE PROMISED THAT SHE'D GIVE HIM AN AUTOMOBILE
   WITH A DIAMOND HEADLIGHT AND A GOLDEN WHEEL.

4. HE HAD A MILLION CATTLE AND A MILLION SHEEP,
   HAD A MILLION VESSELS ON THE OCEAN DEEP,
   HE HAD A MILLION DOLLARS ALL IN FIVES AND TENS,
   HAD A MILLION ROOSTERS AND A MILLION HENS.

5. HE LANDED IN CHICAGO ONE EVENIN' QUITE LATE,
   CALLED HIS SUGAR BABY, SAID "LET'S HAVE A DATE,"
   WILLIE TRIED TO KISS HER, SHE BEGAN TO SHOUT,
   AND THEN HE WOKE UP BECAUSE THE BOOZE GAVE OUT.

Worry, Worry, Worry

BY PLUMBER DAVIS
AND JULES TAUB

(MODERATELY)

1. WELL WOR-RY, WOR-RY, WOR-RY, ___ WOR-RY IS ALL ___ I CAN
2. IT HURT ME SO BAD ___ WHEN YOU SAID ___ THAT WE
3. WELL, SOME-DAY, BA-BY ___ WHEN THE BLOOD ___ RUNS COLD

DO ___ YES, WOR-RY, WOR-RY, WOR-RY, ___
WERE THRU. ___ IT HURT ME SO BAD ___
IN MY VEINS. ___ YES, SOME-DAY, BA-BY ___

WOR-RY IS ALL I CAN DO. ___ YES, MY
WHEN YOU SAID THAT WE WERE THRU. ___ I WOULD
WHEN THE BLOOD RUNS COLD IN MY VEINS. ___ YOU WON'T

LIFE IS SO MIS-ER-'BLE, BA-BY ___ AND IT'S ALL ON AC-COUNT OF
RATH-ER BE DEAD THAN TO BE HERE ___ LONE-SOME AND
BE ABLE TO HURT ME NO MORE ___ 'CAUSE ___ MY HEART WON'T FEEL NO

YOU. ___
BLUE. ___
PAIN. ___

THE WOMAN I LOVE

BY B. B. KING AND
J. JOSEA

THE WORST THING IN MY LIFE

BY B. B. KING AND
J. JOSEA

(MODERATELY)

YES, IT WAS THE WORST THING IN MY LIFE_____ THE

WORST THING I EV·ER WIT·NESSED TO; THE WORST THING IN MY LIFE_____

THE WORST THING I EV·ER WIT·NESSED TO. WHEN THE

WO·MAN THAT I LOVED___ WHEN SHE SAID___ WE WERE REAL·LY THROUGH.

2. TAKE IT EASY BABY
LOTS OF THINGS COME BEFORE WE PART
(REPEAT)
YES LOTS OF THOSE LITTLE THINGS YOU'RE DOING
I WANT TO KNOW IF YOU'RE DOING THEM
BECAUSE YOU THINK YOU'RE SO SMART.

3. I DON'T SAY THAT YOU WON'T LEAVE ME
BUT THINK OF THE SHAPE YOU'LL BE IN
(REPEAT)
I WANT TO KNOW YOU'LL HATE THAT YOU
EVER MET ME
AND YOU'LL HATE THE DAY THAT WE
BEGAN.

4. WHY SHOULD YOU 'CUSE ME, BABY,
WITHOUT ME GIVING YOU A CAUSE
(REPEAT)
I KNOW I'VE BEEN GOOD TO YOU, BABY,
AS IF I WAS A SANTA CLAUS.

5. YOU DON'T THINK MUCH OF YOUR
LIFE
TO PUT YOURSELF IN A SPOT
(REPEAT)
WHEN THE PEOPLE SEE ME CLOWNING
THEY ALL WONDER WHAT YOU GOT.

You Can't Make It

By James Moore
and Roy Hayes

1. A MAN NEEDS A WO·MAN; A WO·MAN NEEDS A MAN; A (CHO.)
SHIP NEEDS A CAP·TAIN; AND I HOPE YOU UN·DER·STAND YOU CAN'T
MAKE IT! ____ YOU CAN'T MAKE IT ON YOUR
OWN! OH, NO! YOU NEED A MAN LIKE ME TO
MAKE YOUR LIFE COM·PLETE! ____

2. A SONG NEEDS A SINGER
A FLOWER NEEDS DEW
A BELL NEEDS A RINGER
AND THAT'S WHY I'M TELLIN' YOU

3. I BRING HOME MY MONEY
EACH AND EVERY WEEK.
THE DAY I SPEND A FEW DOLLARS
THAT NIGHT MY CLOTHES IS IN THE STREET

Your Fool

By B. B. King and
J. Josea

2. YEH, YOU USED TO TREAT ME LIKE A FOOL BABY,
STILL I LOVED EVERYTHING YOU DONE.
I WAS JUST YOUR FOOL, I WAS YOUR FOOL, BABY,
YES IF YOU EVER___ IF YOU EVER LOVE ME, WOMAN,
YES, I TELL YOU BABY.

3. YES, YOU CAN GO AHEAD WITH YOUR ___
AND GET ___ OFF YOUR FACE
YES, YOU'LL NEVER FEEL WHAT I'M FEELING,
AND AT TIMES I DO REALIZE   BABY,
THAT THE ___ IS COMING DOWN THE SIDE.

You're Breaking My Heart

BY B.B. KING AND
J. JOSEA

You're Gonna Miss Me

BY B. B. KING AND
J. TAUB

(MODERATELY FAST)

LET ME TELL YOU PEO-PLE, A LOW-DOWN THING OR TWO

I JUST CAN'T STAND THAT OLD E-VIL WAY SHE DO, YOU'RE GON-NA

miss me ___ You're gon-na miss me ___ You're gon-na

MISS ME, BA-BY, WHEN I'M DEAD AND GONE. ___

2. I CAME HOME THIS MORNING
SHE WOULDN'T LET ME IN
SHE SAID "GO AWAY BABY,
I'VE GOT TOO MANY FRIENDS"
YOU'RE GONNA MISS ME BABY
WHEN I'M DEAD AND GONE.

3. IT'S HARD TO LOVE A WOMAN
WHEN THE WOMAN DON'T LOVE YOU
SHE'LL TREAT YOU SO LOW-DOWN AND DIRTY
TILL YOU DON'T KNOW WHAT TO DO
YOU'RE GONNA MISS ME BABY
WHEN I'M DEAD AND GONE.

4. BYE BYE BABY
I HOPE WE MEET AGAIN
YOU WON'T BE SO EVIL
AND YOU WON'T HAVE SO MANY FRIENDS
YOU'RE GONNA MISS ME, BABY,
WHEN I'M DEAD AND GONE.

You're Too Fast

By Lightnin' Sam Hopkins

too fast, ba-by,   try to

slow down for a-while   you're too   fast, ba-by,

try to slow down for a-while   so that when you

get lost   that's ma-ma's ba-by child.

2) You so fast, baby, old Lightnin' can't understand
   " " " " " " " " " "
   You was so fast when you past me
   I couldn't even catch yo' hand.

WOKE UP THIS MORNING
(MY BABY SHE WAS GONE)

By B. B. KING AND
J. TAUB

(MODERATELY) FAST)

I WOKE UP THIS MORN·IN'_____ MY BA·BY WAS GONE_____
I AIN'T GOT NO BA·BY _____ STAY·IN' HOME WITH ME_____
BA·BY _____ I'M ALL A·LONE_____
BA·BY _____ COME ON STAY WITH ME_____

I WOKE UP THIS MORN·IN'_____ MY BA·BY WAS
I AIN'T GOT NO BA·BY_____ STAY·IN' HOME WITH
BA·BY_____ I'M ALL A·
BA·BY_____ COME ON STAY WITH

GONE_____ I FEEL SO BAD_____
ME_____ MY BABY SHE'S GONE_____
LONE_____ I AIN'T HAD NO LOVIN'_____
ME_____ MY BABY SHE'S GONE_____

I'M ALL A·LONE._____
AND I'M IN MIS·E·RY._____
SINCE MY BA·BY'S BEEN GONE._____
AND I'M IN MIS·E·RY._____